DISCARDED
Queensbury, NY 12804

Opposing Viewpoints®

Gangs

Other Books of Related Interest

Opposing Viewpoints®

Gangs

William Dudley and Louise I. Gerdes, *Book Editors*

Bruce Glassman, *Vice President*
Bonnie Szumski, *Publisher*
Helen Cothran, *Managing Editor*

OPPOSING
VIEWPOINTS®
SERIES

GREENHAVEN PRESS
An imprint of Thomson Gale, a part of The Thomson Corporation

THOMSON

GALE

Detroit • New York • San Francisco • San Diego • New Haven, Conn.
Waterville, Maine • London • Munich

© 2005 Thomson Gale, a part of The Thomson Corporation.

Thomson and Star Logo are trademarks and Gale and Greenhaven Press are registered trademarks used herein under license.

For more information, contact
Greenhaven Press
27500 Drake Rd.
Farmington Hills, MI 48331-3535
Or you can visit our Internet site at http://www.gale.com

ALL RIGHTS RESERVED.
No part of this work covered by the copyright hereon may be reproduced or used in any form or by any means—graphic, electronic, or mechanical, including photocopying, recording, taping, Web distribution or information storage retrieval systems—without the written permission of the publisher.

Every effort has been made to trace the owners of copyrighted material.

Cover credit: © Photodisk

LIBRARY OF CONGRESS CATALOGING-IN-PUBLICATION DATA

Gangs / William Dudley and Louise I. Gerdes, book editors.
    p. cm. — (Opposing viewpoints series)
Includes bibliographical references and index.
ISBN 0-7377-2234-7 (lib. bdg. : alk. paper) —
ISBN 0-7377-2235-5 (pbk. : alk. paper)
    1. Gangs—United States. 2. Juvenile delinquency—United States. I. Dudley, William, 1964– . II. Gerdes, Louise I., 1953– . III. Opposing viewpoints series (Unnumbered)
HV6439.U5G363 2005
364.1'06'60973—dc22   2004052288

Printed in the United States of America

"Congress shall make no law. . . abridging the freedom of speech, or of the press."

First Amendment to the U.S. Constitution

The basic foundation of our democracy is the First Amendment guarantee of freedom of expression. The Opposing Viewpoints Series is dedicated to the concept of this basic freedom and the idea that it is more important to practice it than to enshrine it.

Contents

Why Consider Opposing Viewpoints?

"The only way in which a human being can make some approach to knowing the whole of a subject is by hearing what can be said about it by persons of every variety of opinion and studying all modes in which it can be looked at by every character of mind. No wise man ever acquired his wisdom in any mode but this."

John Stuart Mill

In our media-intensive culture it is not difficult to find differing opinions. Thousands of newspapers and magazines and dozens of radio and television talk shows resound with differing points of view. The difficulty lies in deciding which opinion to agree with and which "experts" seem the most credible. The more inundated we become with differing opinions and claims, the more essential it is to hone critical reading and thinking skills to evaluate these ideas. Opposing Viewpoints books address this problem directly by presenting stimulating debates that can be used to enhance and teach these skills. The varied opinions contained in each book examine many different aspects of a single issue. While examining these conveniently edited opposing views, readers can develop critical thinking skills such as the ability to compare and contrast authors' credibility, facts, argumentation styles, use of persuasive techniques, and other stylistic tools. In short, the Opposing Viewpoints Series is an ideal way to attain the higher-level thinking and reading skills so essential in a culture of diverse and contradictory opinions.

In addition to providing a tool for critical thinking, Opposing Viewpoints books challenge readers to question their own strongly held opinions and assumptions. Most people form their opinions on the basis of upbringing, peer pressure, and personal, cultural, or professional bias. By reading carefully balanced opposing views, readers must directly confront new ideas as well as the opinions of those with whom they disagree. This is not to simplistically argue that everyone who reads opposing views will—or should—change his or her opinion. Instead, the series enhances readers' understanding of their own views by encouraging confrontation with opposing ideas. Careful examination of others' views can lead to the readers' understanding of the logical inconsistencies in their own opinions, perspective on why they hold an opinion, and the consideration of the possibility that their opinion requires further evaluation.

Evaluating Other Opinions

To ensure that this type of examination occurs, Opposing Viewpoints books present all types of opinions. Prominent spokespeople on different sides of each issue as well as well-known professionals from many disciplines challenge the reader. An additional goal of the series is to provide a forum for other, less known, or even unpopular viewpoints. The opinion of an ordinary person who has had to make the decision to cut off life support from a terminally ill relative, for example, may be just as valuable and provide just as much insight as a medical ethicist's professional opinion. The editors have two additional purposes in including these less known views. One, the editors encourage readers to respect others' opinions—even when not enhanced by professional credibility. It is only by reading or listening to and objectively evaluating others' ideas that one can determine whether they are worthy of consideration. Two, the inclusion of such viewpoints encourages the important critical thinking skill of objectively evaluating an author's credentials and bias. This evaluation will illuminate an author's reasons for taking a particular stance on an issue and will aid in readers' evaluation of the author's ideas.

It is our hope that these books will give readers a deeper understanding of the issues debated and an appreciation of the complexity of even seemingly simple issues when good and honest people disagree. This awareness is particularly important in a democratic society such as ours in which people enter into public debate to determine the common good. Those with whom one disagrees should not be regarded as enemies but rather as people whose views deserve careful examination and may shed light on one's own.

Thomas Jefferson once said that "difference of opinion leads to inquiry, and inquiry to truth." Jefferson, a broadly educated man, argued that "if a nation expects to be ignorant and free . . . it expects what never was and never will be." As individuals and as a nation, it is imperative that we consider the opinions of others and examine them with skill and discernment. The Opposing Viewpoints Series is intended to help readers achieve this goal.

David L. Bender and Bruno Leone,
Founders

Greenhaven Press anthologies primarily consist of previously published material taken from a variety of sources, including periodicals, books, scholarly journals, newspapers, government documents, and position papers from private and public organizations. These original sources are often edited for length and to ensure their accessibility for a young adult audience. The anthology editors also change the original titles of these works in order to clearly present the main thesis of each viewpoint and to explicitly indicate the opinion presented in the viewpoint. These alterations are made in consideration of both the reading and comprehension levels of a young adult audience. Every effort is made to ensure that Greenhaven Press accurately reflects the original intent of the authors included in this anthology.

Introduction

"Police officers . . . regularly harass, detain, and photograph youths who are only suspected of—not charged with—gang activity. Police then store that information in computer databases, so they now have files on citizens who have never committed a crime."

—Nina Siegal, human rights journalist

A high school junior, Claudio Ceja of Anaheim, California, spends from 8 A.M to 2:35 P.M. in school, from 4 P.M. to 6 P.M. handing out fliers for a local business, and from 6 P.M. to 9:30 P.M. completing his homework before he goes to his second job at a local convention center. Although Ceja has never been arrested or charged with any crime, over a period of several years, the Anaheim police have stopped, detained, and photographed him five times. Ceja has told the police he is not involved with a gang, yet they take his picture anyway, and his photograph is now in California's gang-tracking computer database, CalGANG. "They seem to be doing it for the fun of it," says Ceja. "They take my picture, and they put it in a gang file. But I'm not a gangster. I don't want to be identified as one."

One of the most controversial tools used to restore communities plagued by gang violence is the tracking of gang members using computer databases. While law enforcement authorities claim gang-tracking databases reduce gang crime and violence, others argue that they unnecessarily harass citizens, particularly minorities who have committed no crimes.

Some of the most well-known gang-tracking databases were developed in California. In 1997, motivated by growing public fears that the gang menace was spreading throughout the state, then-governor Pete Wilson implemented the statewide gang-tracking program, CalGANG, a master database of gang members gathered from over 150 law enforcement agencies throughout the state. Shortly after its development, CalGANG held almost a quarter of a million names, and that number continues to grow. Cal-

GANG's success, as reported by California law enforcement officials, inspired other states to create their own databases.

Gang-tracking databases contain names of alleged gang members and gang associates, together with personal information about each entry. The information entered into a database might include the name of the gang an individual belongs to, his or her home address, identifying marks or tattoos, and photographs. To use the system, gang investigators enter information they have about a suspect thought to have committed a gang-related crime. Information might include a physical description, including the location of tattoos, obtained from a witness. The database responds with a list of matches that investigators can use to round up likely suspects for questioning or create a gallery of mug shots to show witnesses. Cisco Systems, the creator of the secure network on which the CalGANG database is run, maintains that CalGANG is responsible for hundreds of arrests and has helped resolve countless crimes. The database can also determine which communities have the greatest law enforcement needs. According to Wes McBride, former Los Angeles County sheriff's deputy and president and founder of the California Gang Investigators Association, "The ability to produce accurate numbers about gang-related investigations, arrests, and prosecutions makes it easier for the department to get the funding it needs."

Youth advocates, civil rights activists, and others oppose gang-tracking databases for several reasons. One is that the criteria for inclusion in the database are so broad and sweeping that many innocent youth are included. One set of guidelines provides that names should be added to the database if two or more of the following gang criteria are met: the individual professes to being a gang member; is deemed a gang member by a reliable source, such as a trusted informant, teacher, or parent; is called a gang member by an untested informant with corroboration; has gang graffiti on his personal property or clothing; is observed, by an officer, using gang hand signs; hangs around with gang members; or is arrested with gang members.

However, according to law professors Linda S. Beres and Thomas D. Griffith, some of these criteria do not necessarily prove an individual is in a gang. "An individual living in an area with a significant gang presence may find it difficult to avoid 'hanging around' with gang members." They also question the reliability of the information provided by teachers and parents, who are not gang experts. Moreover, many law-abiding young people could be included simply because they wear gang-style clothing. Complicating the problem is the fact that few safeguards exist to prevent being falsely identified as a gang member. According to Beres and Griffith, "Lists are secret; access is denied to the public. Individuals have no right to know that they have been placed on a list. . . . Once entered into a database, it seldom is possible for individuals to get their names removed."

Critics also claim that gang-tracking databases have a disproportionate effect on minorities. "There's a racially discriminatory aspect to all of these programs," claims Ed Chen of the American Civil Liberties Union. "In every case that we've seen, the targets are Latino or African American youth. They concentrate on young black, brown, and sometimes yellow men. It's rarely used against non-minorities," Chen maintains. One study of the 112,000 purported Los Angeles gang members and associates on the CalGANG database revealed that about two-thirds entered were Latinos, about one-third were African American, and only two thousand were Caucasian.

Whether or not gang-tracking databases violate civil liberties or unnecessarily target minority youth remains controversial. The authors in *Opposing Viewpoints: Gangs* submit their views about the gang problem in the following chapters: How Serious Is the Problem of Gangs? What Factors Encourage Gang Behavior? How Can the Legal System Best Reduce Gang Violence? What Can Be Done to Address the Problem of Gangs? As Claudio Ceja's experience illustrates, those researching gang-related problems must examine not only the harm that gangs themselves cause but also the potential dangers associated with measures designed to reduce those harms.

CHAPTER 1

How Serious Is the Problem of Gangs?

Chapter Preface

In order to determine whether or not gangs are a serious threat, analysts from all sides of the debate agree that a definition of gangs and gang-related activity is necessary. Without a definition, they maintain, the extent of the gang problem cannot be accurately measured. Wesley McBride, former Los Angeles County sheriff and president of the California Gang Investigators Association claims, "There is such a disagreement nationwide about exactly what a gang crime is that it has never been counted. . . . If you really wanted to do something about gangs, you would want to know what the real problem is." Indeed, despite the widespread desire to address gang problems, disagreement remains over the definition of gang-related activity. According to journalists Megan Garvey and Richard Winton of the *LA Times*, "the result has been a generation's worth of policy decisions, anti-gang programs and law enforcement initiatives based on social theories and public fear instead of verifiable trends."

Los Angeles is one of several U.S. cities that identifies gangs as a growing menace. In its fight against gang crime, the Los Angeles Police Department (LAPD) defines gang-related crime as any crime committed by a gang member. Critics say that this definition is too broad to be useful and requires police officers to make a subjective determination about which suspects are actually gang members, using criteria such as the wearing of certain colors or being seen with known gang members.

Professor Francine Garcia-Hallcom claims: "Strict adherence to a broad definition obviously creates a gang . . . where perhaps no gang exists at all!" Moreover, she contends, broad definitions can lead to absurd results: "If a youth is arrested while in the company of a known gang member, the errant youngster is considered a gang member as well—and on record! Ironically, the truly anti-social criminal can altogether escape being labeled a gang member by working alone."

The misapplication of the gang label is of particular concern for those who live in states that have harsher punishments for gang-related crime. Critics fear that a broad definition of gang crime will unfairly punish young people who have not committed serious infractions. According to youth advocate Father Gregory Boyle, the broad definition fails to distinguish between crimes committed to help a gang from those committed for personal reasons, such as drug addiction and family arguments. Moreover, Boyle argues, gang-banging falls along a continuum "from writing on the wall, to shooting people up, to getting in their faces." A broad definition of gang-related crime thus metes out severe punishments for both the youth who paints a wall with graffiti and the gang member who murders a rival gang member.

Even strict anti-gang advocates such as Los Angeles mayor James K. Hahn seek a more useful definition, but for different reasons. Hahn believes that gang-related crime may in fact be higher than reported. Hahn claims that many people "don't recognize gang-related crime might be worse than they were counting. . . . It spreads into narcotics, it spreads into domestic violence. I think there was a failure to recognize that gangs were involved in a lot of crimes in the neighborhood beyond drive-by shootings and homicides." Lieutenant Mike Langston of the Aurora, Illinois, Police Department concludes, "By agreeing upon a uniform definition of what constitutes a criminal gang, what describes a person as a member/associate of a gang, and what unlawful acts comprise gang-involved crime, the law enforcement profession can begin the difficult, but not impossible, task of reversing the current menace that has engulfed many of America's young people and their communities."

The debate continues over how gangs and gang-related crime should be defined and thus whether gangs are a serious problem. The authors in the following chapter, while expressing their views on the gravity of the gang problem, inevitably grapple with this problem of definitions.

"The malignancy of the gang presence kills communities just as surely as their bullets kill people."

Gangs Are a Serious Problem in American Communities

Wesley McBride

Gangs are growing in number and sophistication, claims Wesley McBride in the following viewpoint, which was excerpted from testimony given before the U.S. Senate Committee on the Judiciary. Gangs use fear to maintain their power and kill indiscriminately to prevent law-abiding citizens from testifying against them, McBride maintains. To fight these urban terrorists, he argues, those across the nation who fight gang violence must coordinate their efforts. McBride, a former Los Angeles county sheriff, is president of the California Gang Investigators Association.

As you read, consider the following questions:

1. In McBride's view, what is preventing the union of Los Angeles gangs and Chicago-based gangs?
2. According to McBride, what must law enforcement agencies put in place to counter the physical and psychological threats gangs use to discourage potential witnesses against them?
3. In the author's opinion, why is official denial of the gang problem a gang's greatest ally?

Wesley McBride, testimony before the U.S. Senate Committee on the Judiciary, Washington, DC, September 17, 2003.

I would like to thank the [Senate Committee on the Judiciary] for inviting my testimony on the prosecution of criminal street gangs. My name is Wesley D. McBride. I served over 35 years with the Los Angeles County Sheriff's Department obtaining the rank of sergeant and retired on January 31, 2002. I joined the gang unit in 1972, and for the next 28 years of my service, I continuously worked street gang investigations. I served as an intelligence officer, investigator, and team leader. At the time of my retirement, I was the intelligence sergeant for Safe Streets Bureau, Operation Safe Streets (OSS), the Sheriff's Department's gang detail.

By way of introduction and to establish my credentials as a gang investigator, I would like to quickly give you a snapshot of my background.

I am currently the president of the California Gang Investigators Association and am the past president of the National Alliance of Gang Investigators Association, which encompasses all major gang investigators associations, along with representatives of each of the federal law enforcement agencies. I am also the co-author of a textbook on street gangs entitled *Understanding Street Gangs*.

In my various capacities in the gang unit, I have lectured extensively around the nation at various universities and for law enforcement agencies including the Bureau of Investigation's (FBI) National Academy and in-service classes for active Federal agents. I have also testified as an expert gang witness in many criminal cases both in California and outside of the state of California.

I began the development of the Gang Reporting, Evaluation And Tracking (GREAT) computer system and aided in the development of its more advanced replacement system entitled Cal/Gangs. I was a founding member of the California/Federal Committee investigating the development of a multi-state automated gang file system.

Growing in Number and Sophistication

In the nearly three decades that I served in the gang unit, I made an extensive study of gangs, and I must tell you that I have watched the gangs grow in number and sophistication over the years. In Los Angeles County we have hundreds of persons slain every year by gang members. I have watched this number grow from less than two hundred a year to 807 during our record year of 1995. A phenomena that I have observed over this period is that while there have been occasional declines in statistics over the years, these respites are only temporary and soon begin to climb again. The declines never seem to establish a record low; however, the climatic rise at the end of the decline almost always does set a record.

We have over 1,100 gangs in Los Angeles County with a membership of nearly 100,000. These gangs began migrating across this county in the mid-1980s and have established their presence in nearly every state of the union. They freely cross state lines transporting firearms and narcotics, but possibly what may be even more important is that they bring their street gang mentality with them, a mentality that depends on inane gang violence to establish their rule. Los Angeles gangs that migrate into the Eastern U.S. or Midwest are joining forces with the Chicago based gangs with the possibility of uniting into a Super-gang in the future. At the present time the two gang styles are very different in structure and style, thus preventing such a union.

Killing Communities

These gangsters will infect the communities that they settle in with the disease of gangs, a disease that always brings death and desperation with it. The malignancy of the gang presence kills communities just as surely as their bullets kill people. Gangs so intimidate the citizens of communities that they are too afraid to testify or even complain about the gang's activities. The gangs physically threaten and intimidate witnesses as a matter of course. It is not uncommon for them to injure or kill prospective witnesses. It is not uncommon for gangs to attack police who come into conflict with them, and many officers have lost their lives in the war on gangs; however, gangs have even been known to even kill police officers who serve as witnesses against them.

The most important weapon in the gangs' arsenal is fear. Gangs are the master predators of the urban landscape. Their ability to instill fear into the people of a community knows no bounds. They will kill indiscriminately to make their point.

This fear percolates through the community and so underlies all aspects of the gang's activity that it becomes a part of the atmosphere. After a time physical threats are not needed; the threat is unspoken but part of the community culture.

Countering the Threat

To counter this threat strong witness protection programs must be put in place by law enforcement and prosecution agencies. Programs that extend well past the present case that the witness is involved in. These programs need the funding to permanently relocate the witnesses and their families to new communities well away from the one affected by the gang case. Gangsters have a long and unforgiving memory.

Smith. © by North American Syndicate. Reproduced by permission.

Law enforcement responses to gangs have been effective to a degree in various cities around the country. The underlying problem with current law enforcement approaches is that they tend to be crisis driven and short lived in too many cases. There has never been a national coordinated effort to attack the gang problem. There have been effective and deserving programs, but they seem to be isolated in particular locales with little communication outside the affected area.

There has been very little coordination of gang enforcement between local and federal agencies beyond the establishment of a few task forces around the country. There is no effective nationwide database of gang members despite the fact that they travel across the country on a daily basis. There is no standard definition of gangs or gang crimes nationally. No federal agency collects or disseminates gang crime statistics or demographics in order to establish the true picture of gangs. What is done is done by the various Gang Investigators Associations. The National Alliance of Gang Investigators Associations and the National Youth Gang Center has just been awarded a grant to study and publish an assessment of the national threat that gangs present to our country.

The Los Angeles County Sheriff's Department in partnership with the Los Angeles Police Department has . . . formed a multi-jurisdictional street gang-clearing house, known as L.A. Regional Gang Information Network (LARGIN). It will be staffed by officers and analysts from various police jurisdictions and provide daily intelligence data and statistical information enabling law enforcement agencies to tactically plan for anti-gang violence operations and aid investigators in their criminal investigations. A national model could easily be built from this kernel.

Urban Terrorism

I will tell you that the threat of street gangs is a more realistic threat to the people of this country than any threat that external terrorism can make. . . . Many may argue [about] the [application of the] term urban terrorism when speaking of street gangs, but gangs generate community fear and the disillusionment of the communities with local government due to the perceived power of the gangs. When I encounter community people in my travels and lectures, they see and experience the threat of gangs.

Since the [September 11, 2001, terrorist attacks], many gang units have been reassigned to investigate external terrorist threats active within our borders. These investigations are vital; however, they should be in addition to, not instead of the continued investigation of street gangs. One of the disturbing issues that regularly comes to our association from various points across this nation is that the gang units are disappearing and that criteria used to qualify a person as a gang member or an incident as gang involved are being reworked into such narrow parameters that few qualify for gang file. Denial has become a tool of administrators and officials to combat gangs, apparently hoping that they, gangs, will fade away without having to expend resources on them. Denial is the greatest ally the gangs have as it gives them room and time to formulate their takeover of the communities.

There has been no federal leadership in the world of gang enforcement. Gang enforcement still tends to be done by pockets of investigators with little or no communication between these isolated islands.

Prosecution of street gangs based on R.I.C.O. [Racketeer Influenced and Corrupt Organizations] statutes are too time consuming and labor intensive for local gang prosecution. Establishment of R.I.C.O. requirements can take months to years. As an example, in Los Angeles as mentioned there are over 1,100 gangs, 100,000 gang members, hundreds of murders a year, and thousands of violent crimes. One study out of U.S.C. [University of Southern California] states that 10–15 people are shot and wounded for everyone that dies of gunshot wounds. There is an undeterminable amount of narcotic/gang related crime. A few years back a R.I.C.O. prosecution against just one of these gangs took nearly 4 years to complete and took less than 50 people to jail, and less than half were known gang members. Granted those convicted were incarcerated for a very long time, but there was hardly a ripple in the gang violence committed by that gang or for that matter in the gang's activity.

Insistence on using R.I.C.O. many times scares local participation off. Use of specific crimes for quicker prosecution results in more arrests and more public displays of law enforcement action against the gangs. The criminals convicted may not serve the extended incarceration afforded by R.I.C.O. but the time is still significant and public perception is greatly enhanced.

To effectively combat the rise in gangs there must be a multi-faceted approach to prosecution of the gang.

| *"The image of gangs created by the media is not accurate."*

The Media Sensationalize the Gang Problem

Mike Carlie

The media misrepresent the gang problem by focusing on individual gang violence rather than on the social causes that contribute to the formation of gangs, argues Mike Carlie in the following viewpoint, which was excerpted from his book *Into the Abyss: A Personal Journey into the World of Street Gangs.* According to Carlie, the media's obsession with violent crime encourages the public to view the world as a frightening place. By exaggerating gang-related violence, he claims, the media distort the public's view of gangs, making them appear more violent and widespread than they really are. Carlie is professor of sociology and criminal justice at Southwest Missouri State University, in Springfield.

As you read, consider the following questions:

1. According to Carlie, why does television influence how people define reality?
2. In the author's opinion, for what can gang members thank media portrayals of their activities?
3. What is the contagion effect, in the author's view?

Mike Carlie, *Into the Abyss: A Personal Journey into the World of Street Gangs.* Springfield, MO: Self Publication, 2002. Copyright © 2002 by Michael K. Carlie. All rights reserved. Reproduced by permission.

What you and I perceive of as "reality" is, in many ways, a social construct. Other people and the media create images in our minds as to what is real. As to the role of other people, [R.C.] Surette tells us that "People create reality—the world they believe exists—based on their individual knowledge and from knowledge gained from social interactions with other people." [According to Surette,]

> Television viewing constantly ranks as the third most time-consuming activity (after sleep and work or school) for Americans. Americans spend nearly half of their free time watching television and television today is a more consuming socializing agent than school and church combined.

Americans watch a great deal of television and often base their perception of the world upon media content. How the media define reality is how many observers then define reality. This is not surprising given the extent of electronic socialization to which most youth are exposed today.

According to Surette, "Public surveys have reported that as many as 95 percent of the general population cite the mass media as their primary source of information about crime." To some extent, then reality is what other people and the media tell us it is. [According to David Starbuck, James C. Howell, and Donna T. Linquist,]

> The public continues to perceive youth gangs and gang members in terms of the media stereotype of the California Crips and Bloods rather than in terms of current scientific data.

A Distorted View of Crime

What is the media telling us about crime? Do media portrayals accurately reflect the reality of crime or are they a misrepresentation of it? The answer to that question probably lies somewhere between the two. . . .

Media sensationalism, although it sells more advertising and increases the income of the media businesses, is a disservice to the community. In order to deal effectively with a local gang situation, the community must have accurate information, not media hype. [Surette explains,]

> The entertainment media's pattern with regard to portraying crime and justice can be summarized as follows: Whatever the media show is the opposite of what is true. Whatever the

25

truth about crime and violence and the criminal justice system in America, the entertainment media seem determined to project the opposite. The lack of realistic information further mystifies the criminal justice system, exacerbating the public's lack of understanding of it while constructing a perverse topsy-turvy reality of it.

In the end, the point I will try to make is that the social policies we have adopted for dealing with gangs (arrest and incarcerate) are the result of a public perception of gangs which is incorrect—or, at the least, muddled, confused, and misleading. Some of the responsibility for this belongs to the media.

Media Images of Crime and Gangs

[J. Hagedorn states,] "Our view of gangs is still mainly shaped by the media and law enforcement, who typically define gangs as organized crime."

To my knowledge, no studies have yet been published which investigate the impact of media presentations on public attitudes about *gangs*. There have, however, been reports of the devastating impact of negative reportage on certain ethnic groups. A Melbourne, Australia, study concerned with media portrayals of Vietnamese young people (VYP) and the impact the portrayals had upon them, [according to S. Leiber and H. Rodd,] "their Vietnamese community, and the . . . community in general" may serve as an example. [They write,]

> From 1994–1996 residents in the Inner Western suburbs of Melbourne . . . were bombarded with local newspaper reports of "youth violence," "youth drug dealing," "Asian gangs" and "youth crime." Most of these reports targeted Vietnamese young people as the culprits, tapping into two of the wider community's underlying fears and prejudices: their suspicion of young people and their fear of difference.

> Street kids, Asians, heroin, gambling, knives, gangs and crime became big news. Consequently, the larger Melbourne dailies, talkback [talk shows], even "A Current Affair" [television program] picked up on the drama and controversy. The frenzy of such reportage conveyed a sense of impending threat and utter crisis. It sparked a police crackdown; it had them declaring "war" and it had local traders hiring security staff. We saw references to Los Angeles by local community members, followed by the Pennington Drug Advisory Council.

> The effect of such sensationalist, simplistic reportage has

been far reaching, devastating and divisive for VYP and the wider Vietnamese community, as well as the general community. . . . Local young people were left stunned, particularly VYP. The representations they saw in the media were far from the reality they lived.

The impact of negative media reportage on these three groupings has been far reaching. It has added to existing division, isolation and defensiveness between them and the rest of the Melbourne community.

There have been many studies concerning the impact of the media on public perceptions of crime and justice. As Surette found, most television entertainment programming sensationalizes and misinforms. [Surette explains,]

Television entertainment largely ignores most aspects of real crime in America, focusing instead on the most serious, violent and life-threatening offenses. By sensationalizing crime in this way, TV misses its opportunity to educate the audience about the true dimensions of America's crime problem.

The Media Obsession with Violent Crime

Take, for example, the media's obsession with rape and murder. Long ago the Federal Bureau of Investigation created a category of crimes known as Index Crimes. The Index Crimes consist of four crimes against persons (murder, rape, robbery, and aggravated assault) and four crimes against property (burglary, larceny/theft, motor vehicle theft, and arson). There are other crimes people commit, to be sure, but those eight are the Index Crimes (used—like the Dow Jones is used for the stock market—as an indicator of whether crime in the United States is going up or down in any given year).

In 2001, rape and murder *combined* accounted for less than .7% (that's *less than one percent*) of *all* Index Crimes known to the police. They would be an even smaller proportion of *all* crimes since not all crimes are included in the Index. To accurately reflect the reality of rape and murder, then, fewer than 7 out of every 1000 crime-related news stories, movies, or television shows should deal with rape and murder. Instead, we are bombarded by one media presentation after another dealing with rape or murder to the near exclusion of the other 99.3% of all Index crimes.

As a result of this distortion of reality, the image created in the mind of the public is that we live in a very scary place where violent crimes are happening all the time and everywhere. According to Surette, "People today live in two worlds: a real world and a media world." The media world is the world created in the mind of viewers as defined by media portrayals. "Such a portrait of the world has been associated with the development of a 'mean worldview'—the feeling that the world is a violent, dangerous place—and attitudes of fear, isolation, and suspicion," [Surette says.]

Inaccurate Media Portrayals

A youth gang is a group of three or more youths whose members routinely commit serious crimes and regularly engage in severe acts of violence. The media's inaccurate usage of the term gang does real harm to all youth, in particular to visible minority youth. More often than not, the media present black youth as being representative of all gang members. Although racial origin is an important factor in gang analysis, the media do not offer any thought or analysis as to why this may be the case. For example, visible minority youths face discrimination in many areas of their lives and as a result, experience blocked opportunities in the areas of schooling and employment. In the face of this, gangs have more appeal.

Mark Totten, *Ottawa Citizen*, February 10, 1999.

There are gang members who watch the news and listen to the radio. They go to the movies, read newspapers, magazines, and journals, and they surf the Internet. Media mention of their activities furthers their purposes. A frightened public is an easy target. Rather than having to intimidate the public themselves, gang members can thank the media for taking care of that for them.

For the sake of argument, I will suggest the impact of media portrayals of crime and criminality on the American public's perception of them are similar to the impact of media portrayals of gangs—distorted, sensationalized, and self-serving.

Fractured Realities

[Surette writes,] The repeated message in the visual entertainment media (film and television) is that crime is largely perpetrated by individuals who are basically different from the majority, that criminality stems from individual problems, and that criminal conduct is freely chosen behavior.

In the entertainment media (movies, videos, and television) one may note that, [according to Surette,]

> . . . crime is separated and isolated from other social problems that in reality tend to come bundled together—crime, poverty, unemployment, poor health, poor schools, high divorce rates, high pregnancy rates, community decay and deterioration, illiteracy, drop-out rates, and so on.

The problem is that these social problems *are* linked. By failing to show them together, the viewing public has difficulty making the necessary connections between them. Media portrayals of crime and gangs as *being* the problem rather than being *symptoms* of the problems which cause them to form, are terribly misleading. . . .

Gangs form in response to the collapse of social institutions in the neighborhoods and communities in which they are found. The two—gangs and our social institutions—are inextricably intertwined. The media seldom portray that relationship accurately. Media generated responses of arresting and incarcerating gang members will not reduce gang activity as effectively and permanently as would reducing the poverty, urban decay, poor schooling, substance abuse, and child abuse which contribute so significantly to the formation of gangs.

I don't mean to suggest that criminals, and gang members among them, should not be held responsible for the illegal acts they commit. They should be held responsible and should face certain and appropriate punishment and/or treatment. But to only punish or treat *them* is to continue cleaning up the spill without paying any attention to turning off the spigot.

In light of these comments, limited to a [as Surette puts it] "simplistic, incomplete picture of crime as mostly individual, socially isolated acts, members of each group involved (criminals, crime fighters, and the public) have for generations been receiving a misleading constructed reality in how to engage in and respond to crime.". . .

[Surette explains,] "For every American who is victimized by crime, several experience crime vicariously each evening on their television sets."

There is a contagion effect related to media portrayals of crime and gangs. That is, after an incident occurs in one community and is reported in other communities, people in the other communities respond to the event as if it happened in their own community.

One week before my research sabbatical began there was a fatal gang-related stabbing in a neighboring community about 50 miles from my home. The event dominated the news in my community for more than a week. The perpetrator of the crime was a documented gang member from a city in another state.

The incident turned into the primary topic of conversation on our community's television- and radio talk shows every day for over a week. Daily newspaper editorials added to the frenzy of fear, anger, and concern among the population. Due to the amount of attention the incident received in the media, it almost seemed as though it had happened in my town.

The gang-related murder in a community north of my town happened in *that* community, not in mine nor in any of the approximately 50 communities within range of the media coverage of the event. Mixed with the hype may have been a genuine concern of some in the media who want the public to know what's happening—no matter where it happens. But done to excess, the motivation appears more to be the desire to increase viewership or sales.

The Media and Social Policy

[According to Surette,] "People . . . act in accordance with their constructed view of reality."

If the public perception of gangs is inaccurate, policies designed to address the gang situation based upon that perception are likely to fail. If the perception of gangs is that their members are mostly African-Americans, then we overlook the tragedies occurring in Hispanic, Asian, Russian, Samoan, and other ethnic enclaves in cities throughout America. If the perception is that all gang members are male, then we overlook policies needed to help females stay out of gangs.

If our perception is that all gang members are violent and are "packing" or "strapped" (carrying a gun), then we will support the use of force in dealing with them. The police will have permission to apply the screws. The problem is that not all gang members are violent or armed. . . . Acts of violence by a gang sometimes lead some gang members to leave the gang.

If we think that all gangs and their members are into drugs and that the drug problem is a gang problem, then we not only overlook the tens of thousands of gang members who are not into drugs, we also overlook the drug dealers who are not gang members.

The image of gangs created by the media is not accurate. I'm no different than anyone else and my own experience . . . was that the image I had of gangs wasn't even close to the reality of the situation. It is the inaccurate image, however, which informs public opinion and lays the foundation for our social policies towards gangs. It is no wonder that our current policy of suppression (arrest and incarcerate) hasn't been effective. The image created by the media is that the individual gang member is the problem, not the product of the problem. The gang problem has been incorrectly defined, so our solutions are doomed to failure.

Social policy on how to deal with gangs and their members must be based on a rational assessment of each community's local situation. The media do not contribute constructively to this understanding when they sensationalize gang-related events. On the other hand, when the media undertake to provide documentaries and other thoughtful programs, their efforts can contribute to reducing gang activity. This pro-social aspect of the broadcast and print media should not be overlooked. It should be encouraged and strengthened.

Media programs which focus on the reality of the gang situation in specific communities may stimulate the public to support or develop appropriate policies including all *three* approaches to the gang situation—prevention, intervention, and suppression.

"No city, town, or neighborhood is totally immune from the threat of gangs."

Gang Migration from Large Cities Is a Serious Problem

David M. Allender

In the following viewpoint David M. Allender argues that no American community is immune to the influence of inner-city gangs. Allender has seen signs that West Coast and Chicago gangs have migrated to Indianapolis, for example. Gangs migrate to smaller cities for several reasons, Allender maintains. Some want to deliberately expand their criminal endeavors. In other cases, teenagers living in smaller communities want to imitate romanticized media portrayals of gang life and seek out gang members who move to their area for aid in organizing a gang. Allender is a lieutenant in the Indianapolis, Indiana, Police Department.

As you read, consider the following questions:

1. In Allender's opinion, how does reality contradict media portrayals of inner-city gangs?
2. According to Allender, what two problems arise after the arrest of gang members who spread by the "imperialist method"?
3. In the author's view, what motivated the People Nation gang to form in Chicago?

David M. Allender, "Gangs in Middle America: Are They a Threat?" *FBI Law Enforcement Bulletin*, vol. 70, December 2001. Copyright © 2001 by *FBI Law Enforcement Bulletin*. Reproduced by permission.

In the past 30 years, changes have occurred in how the police and the public view, define, and discuss gangs. In the late 1960s and early 1970s, police in large cities generally acknowledged the existence of gang activity within their jurisdictions. During the 1970s, the public was recovering from the Vietnam War and dealing with a wide variety of important social issues and changes. Gangs and crime did not demand the same attention as these other matters.

An Increased Interest in Gangs

By the middle of the 1980s, however, the public became increasingly concerned with safety issues. The interest continued into the 1990s, partially due to an aging population. In response to the electorates' concern, federal grant programs and monies proliferated. Several of these projects, such as Operation Weed and Seed and the Office of Community-Oriented Policing Services (COPS) antigang initiative, had as a core ingredient the need to control or dismantle criminal street gangs. Increased attention and discussion also brought new legislation to deal with the gangs. Many states enacted statutes to assist police and prosecutors and mandated that new police officers attending basic police academies receive at least a minimal amount of training in gang topics. Media interest mirrored audience appetite and boosted coverage of gang-related subject matter. Increased reporting of such incidents had the effect of making it appear that gang activity was on the rise. But, is this truly the case, especially in middle America? Are states, such as Indiana, "the crossroads of America," at risk of becoming infected with the gang menace or has it occurred already?

An examination of gang history, gang migration, and gang structure, along with the efforts of law enforcement to combat and prevent gangs may provide some answers. In addition, a review of Indianapolis, Indiana's experience with gangs illustrates how a "big small town" in the heart of the United States can become a new target for gangs from other areas of the country. . . .

The most visible criminal street gangs operate in the nation's inner cities. When depicted by either the news media or the entertainment industry, these groups have almost exclusively young black or Hispanic males as members, often portrayed as violent and prosperous because of their involvement in the drug trade. In reality, not all street gangs are involved heavily in drug trafficking; very few street gang members are prosperous; and no shortage of white male gang members exists in inner-city, suburban, or rural areas. Moreover, females often join the gang subculture for the same reasons males do. They may link themselves to a male-dominated gang, or, in some cases, form their own associations. The urban legend about prosperity has grown, however, and many young people see the street gang as a method of achieving both financial and social success. Unfortunately, a few gangsters involved with street gangs are successful, both financially and socially. They become role models to less fortunate young people who are shortsighted and fail to realize the danger and the damage criminal gang activity can do to them, their families, and their neighborhoods.

How Do Gangs Spread?

Criminal street gangs can spread by what some have labeled the "imperialist method." A large street gang will dispatch members to start a chapter in a new city or neighborhood to further some form of criminal activity. For example, in 1999, the Indianapolis Safe Streets Task Force concluded a multi-year investigation of a drug-dealing gang called the New Breed. This gang arrived as an established enterprise from Chicago and only allowed local residents to fill lower levels of the organization. Members would rotate between Chicago, Indianapolis, and at least six other cities. The group had a set of rules and a belief system, which they brought with them. At the conclusion of the investigation, 15 gang members were charged with federal drug trafficking offenses, based on crimes committed in Indianapolis. Numerous New Breed members operating in other cities were unaffected by this case. Two problems arise from this type of gang movement. First, surviving gang members in other locations will, after modifying their methods, move to fill the void left by those arrested. Second, local residents who were either gang members or associates will recreate the operation to take advantage of the available profits. . . . Both of these situations may be occurring in Indianapolis.

Another way an established street gang can spread its influence can be referred to as "franchising." Often done to realize a profit from criminal activity, this method calls for an existing gang to contact local residents and recruit them into the enterprise. If, for example, a Chicago-based gang, such as the Four Corner Hustlers, develops contacts that they trust in Indianapolis, they may work an arrangement to supply drugs in exchange for a substantial share of the profits. Both groups benefit—the locals get a dependable supply of product, and, in this example, the Four Corner Hustlers realize a profit with minimal risk. Most prevalent in drug-dealing enterprises, franchising also can involve such crimes as theft, forgery, or fencing stolen goods.

The Distribution of Gangs

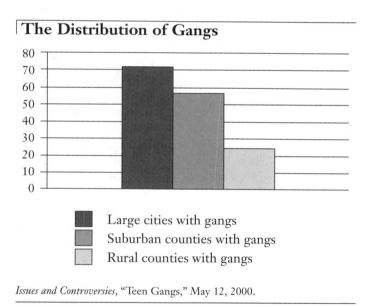

Large cities with gangs
Suburban counties with gangs
Rural counties with gangs

Issues and Controversies, "Teen Gangs," May 12, 2000.

A new street gang often will form because young people have an interest in the gang lifestyle and will look for sources of information. If possible, the curious will find someone who was, or claims to have been, a gang member in another location (e.g., a young person who recently moved into the area from a city, such as Chicago or Los Angeles). This person now becomes the resident "gang expert," and the gang will shape its structure and rules by this person's information. In addition, gang members and their associates watch movies and television programs depicting gang life from which they convert information for their purposes. Conversations with former gang members revealed that they also viewed television news reports, read news stories, and watched reality-based television programs to see how gangs in other places operated. Finally, the Internet represents an important source for emerging gangs. Simply by searching the word *gang*, the inquirer can receive a wealth of Web sites, as well as several chat rooms for gang members. Such numerous and varied sources, many of which give conflicting information, account for the wide diversity in street gang structure and methods of operation.

Examining Gang Structure

Just as there are numerous gangs for aspiring gangsters to imitate, uncounted sources of information exist on how to establish, structure, and rule a street gang. East Coast and Hispanic gangs generate some interest, but the dominant influences in the Midwest are from the West Coast, especially Los Angeles, and from the Chicago area. Observers also will encounter other types of criminal gangs throughout the area, including prison groups, outlaw motorcycle clubs, as well as Asian criminal enterprises and ethnic street gangs. Perhaps, the most recognizable of these latter sets are the outlaw bikers because of their attire, community activities, and Web sites. However, their sophistication and secretive nature concerning their operations and structure prevent the average street gang member from obtaining enough information to imitate them.

In the 1980s, West Coast black gangs formed two loose confederations—the largest, the Crips, and their rivals, the Bloods. Contrary to what many believe, there is neither one Crip nor one Blood gang. Rather, numerous sets of each have joined together to either protect themselves or facilitate their criminal activities. These represent two of the Four Nations. The other two originate from Chicago. In the late 1970s, a very large criminal street gang, known as the Gangster Disciples, formed a coalition with several other street gangs to maximize drug profits and protect their members from violence perpetrated by rivals. The consolidation called itself the Folk Nation. Other gang sets in Chicago felt the need to form an alliance to ensure their share of the drug market. Led by the Vice Lords and the El Rukins, this band dubbed themselves the People Nation, thus creating the big four street gang nations, in no particular order of influence, the Crips, Bloods, Folks, and People.

Sending the Gang Message

In Indianapolis, the West Coast message from the Crip and Blood Nations arrives through a variety of mediums. Evidence shows that a few California area gang members have migrated to Indianapolis. Authorities speculate that these gangsters came to the city to spread their illegal enterprises. However, officials have not documented this nor have they determined if the gangs sent these people to the Midwest or if the gangsters are acting from personal interests. The more common means of transmission for West Coast ideas and models come from the entertainment industry, including music artists who encourage violence and gang values; movies glorifying gangs and their lifestyle; and books, television programs, the Internet, and the news media all publicizing the gang subculture.

Many Indianapolis residents look to Chicago for important legitimate influences, such as business, cultural pursuits, and sports teams. Many people have friends and relatives living in the Chicago area and frequently travel between the cities. With these active methods of communication present, information concerning the gang subculture often occurs by word of mouth. The closeness enables Chicago gangs to exert a measure of control over some of those operating in Indianapolis. For these reasons, the Folk and People Nations dominate the Indianapolis gang landscape, confirmed by area street gang graffiti almost exclusively composed of Chicago-area gang names and symbols. . . .

Preventing Gangs from Taking Hold

No city, town, or neighborhood is totally immune from the threat of gangs. The first step in prevention is for those in authority to study the underlying reasons for gang forma-tion—structure, nurturing, need to belong, economic op-portunity, and excitement. If communities meet these needs, gangs will have a hard time establishing a foothold. How-ever, once gang involvement is suspected, authorities must take time to study the situation to determine the extent and type of problem they need to deal with. A variety of social and law enforcement agencies need to become involved in the discussion process from the beginning. Police and com-munity members need to arrive at a consensus of how seri-ous the gang problem is and then work together to combat any criminal activity.

The police must act as the point group to bring an oper-ating criminal street gang under control. Officers must tar-get the gang in a variety of ways, including the criminal ac-tivities normally associated with the gang. Less apparent, but just as important, is the need to deal with other criminal and antisocial actions on the part of gang members. Officers also should develop strong working relationships with prosecu-tors and probation officers so that, when arrested, gang members receive special attention and appropriate sen-tences. Finally, a standardized reporting system to capture the true extent of gang activity in America remains a goal that all concerned citizens should work toward. Protecting this nation's youth from the dangers of gang involvement re-quires the effort of all facets of the society. If America's heartland is facing the threat of gangs, the entire country is at risk.

"Intelligence gathered from outside law enforcement jurisdictions . . . soon transformed evidence of illicit drugs into possibilities of gang invasions."

Gang Experts Exaggerate the Threat of Gang Migration from Large Cities

Diane Schaefer

Based on information provided by gang experts from large urban areas, law enforcement in smaller communities often misinterpret typical youth behavior, such as wearing baggy clothes, as evidence of an emerging gang problem, claims Diane Schaefer in the following viewpoint. To prove her hypothesis, Schaefer studied an alleged gang invasion in Bloomington, Indiana. Shortly after the arrest of several drug dealers, the Bloomington police were told by big-city gang experts that Bloomington's drug problem was a gang problem. However, real evidence of a gang invasion, such as arrests of gang members for committing violent crimes, never suffered, Schaefer maintains. It would appear, she notes, that Bloomington's gang problem was invented. Schaefer teaches criminology at Eastern Illinois University, at Charleston.

As you read, consider the following questions:

1. In Schaefer's view, what happens when police embrace crime myths?
2. According to Schaefer, what did empirical evidence show was predictive of gang violence?

Diane Schaefer, "Police Gang Intelligence Infiltrates a Small City," *Social Science Journal*, vol. 39, January 2002, p. 95. Copyright © 2002 by JAI Press, Inc. Reproduced by permission of Elsevier, Ltd.

Although nationwide surveys document the existence of gangs throughout America, research on gangs continues mainly in large, metropolitan areas. [R.A.] Weisheit, [D.N.] Falcone, and [L.E.] Wells noted that "[C.R.] Huff's comprehensive collection of contemporary gang research includes no discussion of gangs in smaller cities and rural areas" and questioned whether the spread of gangs into America's heartland is "as real and pervasive as it seems." They suggested "public alarm and awareness" as a possibility for the apparent increase in small city gangs while law enforcement officials discussed a drug-motivated gang migration. This paper investigates the role played by the spread of ideas about gangs from large police jurisdictions to smaller ones.

Studying Gang Migration

Using newspaper reports, law enforcement documents, and other archival data, I portray the emergence of gangs as a law enforcement problem in one small, midwest city. The purpose of this paper is to investigate whether the discovery of gangs in Bloomington, Indiana, resulted from a migration of urban gang members, as police claimed, or from the spread of gang intelligence from outside police departments. . . .

Stereotypes and Myths

Although research now finds few gang migrants in small cities related to an organized drug trade, police stereotypes of drug-related gang infiltrations existed at the beginning of Bloomington's history with gangs. In 1992, the Associated Press discussed police accounts of "gang-related activity [that] has spread from big cities into Indiana's small towns and rural areas." An Indiana State Police gang expert said gangs migrated along interstate routes in order to expand their drug markets. A 1997 CNN news release suggested that this stereotype about drug-dealing gang migrants may occasionally still be invoked. Senator Orrin Hatch remarked, "The territorial expansion of gangs show [sic] they now resemble organized-crime syndicates more than small, romanticized neighborhood street toughs, like those once portrayed in 'West Side Story.'" Crime stereotypes, of course, are not limited to gangs, [E.] Lotke discussed stereotyped images of sex offenders as incurable predators when research indicated negligible recidivism once convicted and/or treated. Still, the myth persisted and served politicians in winning support from voters who received media myths but not realities. The perpetuation of crime myths also serve police.

When police embrace crime myths, mundane occurrences can become subversive dangers. For example, police transformed reports of livestock killed by natural predators into satanic mutilations. Lack of satanic-related crime evidence did not deter police from creating and then spreading a satanic crime model among their colleagues. As with cults, much information about gangs spreads from police in one area to police in other areas via seminars, conferences, and the Internet. Much of this information focuses on noncriminal indicators. In Bloomington, Indiana, police learned to focus on noncriminal indicators of gangs after hearing what police in other jurisdictions said about gangs. An Indiana University Police Lieutenant explained how he learned about gang indicators, such as earrings and haircuts, from Indianapolis officers: "According to information we've received from the Metropolitan gang task force in Indianapolis about the identifying colors, jackets, earrings, tattoos, hats and haircuts of big city gangs, we are certain there is gang activity on campus." Bloomington Police also mentioned learning about gang clothing and colors from outside police agencies. According to an internal memorandum, officers in late summer 1992 "started noticing youth wearing blue bandanna's [sic], sports logo caps (on sideways) and large oversized sports logo clothes which would be consistent with gang apparel that we had received in training from other departments."

Research conducted in other cities confirms that police perceptions of gangs often rely on symbols rather than on crime. According to [J.F.] Quinn and [B.] Downs, police measure the severity of gang problems in smaller cities based mainly on noncriminal indicators, such as a gang's size and organizational sophistication. In fact, "What is both clear and startling . . . is the lack of effect that the frequency of various types of crime have upon the perception of a serious gang problem." Police in smaller jurisdictions rely more on

41

symbols of gangs than on gang crime.

Myths about gang crime also prevail over realities. Gang violence was interpreted as a sign of a gang's involvement in the drug trade, although research did not provide strong support for this connection. Empirical evidence showed instrumental property crimes rather than the drug trade to be predictive of gang violence. Similarly, [C.R.] Block and [R.] Block found turf battles, rather than drugs, as the main cause of gang violence. [M.] Felson concluded that "even law enforcement has played a role in nurturing the image of juvenile gangs as coherent, ruthless groups" and called this social construction the "juvenile gang fallacy." Still, crime myths about dangerous, drug-dealing gangsters prevail over crime realities and shape law enforcement perceptions of gang problems. Quinn and Downs speculated that police accounts of gangs could influence antigang attitudes in other officers, making them "more likely to identify problematic groups as 'gangs'." This labeling process, as well as "the origins of police perceptions," require further investigation. My research takes a step in this direction by outlining how police in Bloomington, Indiana, formed their gang perceptions at the beginning of Bloomington's history with gangs.

The Consequences of Gang-Crime Definitions

Defining a situation as threatening, even when there is little or no evidence to do so, produces real consequences. Police define themselves as a "thin blue line" separating the law-abiding from the criminal while defining gang members "as diametrically opposed" to police and as a threat to the moral and social order. This definition makes gangs suspect especially to urban police. Undergirded by today's wars on crime, police suspicions are readily accepted as accurate. Wars emphasize crime control rather than legal due process even when they may be based primarily on myths rather than realities, on symbols rather than evidence. According to [W.J.] Chambliss and [R.B.] Seidman, such a climate means "the police are probably operating with extra severity against these groups [poor minorities]." Indeed, . . . challenges to police conduct (i.e., the officers on trial for the 1999 Bronx shooting death of Amadou Diallo and investigations into the conduct of LAPD's [Los Angeles Police Department's] CRASH or Community Resources Against Street Hoodlums gang unit) indicated the use of excessive force against urban minorities, especially those suspected of gang activity.

According to [A.] Turk, coercive enforcement of laws occurs when police perceive disenfranchised groups as equally powerful, as potential threats to the status quo. Typically, disinherited groups submit to informal social-control techniques while inequalities stemming from differential access to legislative power remain hidden and unchallenged. When coercion becomes increasingly necessary, it is a sign that those to whom the force is applied refuse to acknowledge the legitimacy and authority of the state. It is a sign of increasing instability in the social order. In light of this, it is particularly disconcerting that today's police war on gangs may be fueled by mythical beliefs and definitions. If this is the case, then the police unnecessarily threaten the social order when they demonize and then antagonize groups who respond by refusing to recognize police (state) authority. When such police wars on crime are egalitarian, as they were in Bloomington where all citizens were suspect, their detrimental effect on civil and democratic social order is undeniable.

Questioning the Gang Problem

Bloomington, Indiana, is located about 60 miles southwest of the state capital, Indianapolis. The city's 1990 Census population was 60,633, which included 29,886 university students. Over half (57.9%) of the town's households earned less than $25,000 per year, which was substantially higher than the national figure of 43.1% and reflected its large student population. There is a pronounced separation of social classes in the city with low-income residents on the west side and the more affluent on the east. Bloomington, however, contains no concentrated pockets of poverty like those characteristic of large, urban centers. According to the 1990 Census, 91.29% of the population was European American, slightly higher than the state's overall percentage of 90.56%. However, compared to the national figure of 71.5% European American and a central city figure of 66%, minorities formed a very small part of Bloomington's population.

The role played by outside police in the formation of Bloomington's gang problem became apparent as I studied the city's gang history as documented in *The* [Bloomington, Indiana] *Herald-Times* newspaper, minutes of meetings of the task force on gangs, videotapes of youth forums, and some police documents. Interviews with police, gang members, and city officials, as well as participant observation at meetings of the task force on gangs, deepened my understanding of this small city's gang problem. . . . I rely heavily on archival data, particularly the local newspaper. Reliance on archival data has two benefits. First, newspaper and other secondary data sources provide an account of Bloomington's gang history as it unfolded while interviews, conducted years later, were less reliable because they depended on an individual's recall of past events. Second, I wanted to understand the context in which gangs developed in Bloomington. Therefore, I studied Bloomington's daily history as recorded in the newspaper rather than just the news about gangs. Unexpectedly, I discovered the vital role played by police and other officials in the emergence of the city's gang problem. The creation of a gang problem, as with any other social problem, is an interactive event occurring within a certain historical context. Studying Bloomington as a whole, rather than focusing on news or data about gangs, highlighted the role of other events in shaping this crime problem.

Inventing an Invasion

In the Fall of 1991, Bloomington's police arrested drug dealers and learned to suspect the presence of gang members, thereby marking the beginning of the city's history with gangs. . . .

At the beginning of Bloomington's history with gangs, police and media wavered between discussing actual arrests of drug dealers and learned fears about possible gang members. Initial news accounts emphasized evidence of a crack problem that included the arrest of two cocaine dealers found in an Indiana University (IU) football player's apartment. Police intelligence gathered directly from these arrests emphasized drugs but not gangs.

Intelligence gathered from outside law enforcement jurisdictions, however, soon transformed evidence of illicit drugs into possibilities of gang invasions. A police officer from Fort Wayne, Indiana, said gangs moved in there "seemingly overnight" and an officer from Anderson, Indiana, lamented that police "simply waited too long" before dealing with Anderson's gang problem. As a result of their experiences with gangs, Anderson officers told Bloomington Police that "Bloomington should waste no time in preparing for the gangs' arrival." This outside advice prompted Bloomington's police and mayor to "map out a plan for repelling gangs." At the beginning of Bloomington's history with gangs, the police obtained evidence of a crack problem and received accounts about a gang threat. . . .

The Advice of Gang Experts

A transition from the arrests of drug dealers to police fears about gangs emerged in two of the three remaining articles. One of these articles drew on material from the Indianapolis Metropolitan gang task force and told the reader how to help "thwart gang proliferation" in Bloomington. The second article featured the comments of an Indianapolis, Indiana, gang task force commander who stated, "You are going to have gangs in Bloomington." Bloomington's police no longer discussed actual drug crimes but addressed the possibility of gang members and responded to this incoming missive about a future gang invasion with anecdotal accounts of a growing gang menace. For example, a Bloomington public-housing security guard said, "I've spoken with a number of present and former gang members. They tell me gang members from Fort Wayne, Detroit and Chicago are in Bloomington right now, and are recruiting new members." The county's juvenile probation supervisor said a former Indianapolis Vice Lord "clearly indicated to us that the Vice Lords and Disciples have targeted Bloomington, and are recruiting young people right now." The local narcotics strike force had a videotape of an intoxicated man who informants identified as, "one of two inner city drug dealers who were ready to go to war over a territorial dispute," thereby conjuring up the image of inner city gang rivalries. Prompted by an Indianapolis gang expert, local criminal justice personnel no longer discussed arrests but relayed stories told by individuals claiming gang affiliation.

The Indianapolis gang expert also outlined four "key indicators" of a gang infiltration: gang-related graffiti, an increased number of young people with weapons, more violent crime, and drive-by shootings. Individuals in Bloomington's criminal justice system responded with more indirect evidence of a large gang presence. A security guard saw "spray-painted graffiti [that] features specific signs and symbols associated with the Vice Lords, Hellraisers, Black Gangster Disciples and Latin Kings." Stories about gang arsenals, the second indicator of gangs, surfaced: "Former [gang] members have told the Bloomington Police there are dozens of gang members already living in Bloomington, most of whom are mined with 0.380s, 0.357s and ouzi [sic] machine guns." The probation department's juvenile division supervisor insisted, "There's definitely been an increase in the number of handgun carryings" and conjectured that local teens needed "to protect themselves from gangs." These criminal justice stories about weapons, however, seem mythical given that adult and juvenile Uniform Crime Report data revealed only one weapons violation in the county for that year (1991).

Dubious Evidence, Faulty Conclusions

Deeply imbedded within the twin contexts of gang proliferation and drug market expansion is public concern about gang migration—the movement of gang members from one city to another. That concern is reflected in the reports of State legislative task force investigations; government-sponsored conferences; and law enforcement accounts at the local, State, and Federal levels. In these documents the evidence cited is most often anecdotal, rarely the result of a systematic assessment of the prevalence, nature, and consequences of gang migration.

With a single exception, the findings of research on this topic contrast sharply with the perspective presented in the government and law enforcement reports as well as in the media. These research studies show that the impact of gang migration is far less than has been believed.

Cheryl L. Maxson, Kristi J. Woods, and Malcolm W. Klein, *National Institute of Justice Journal*, February 1996.

As for the third indicator of a gang presence, Bloomington's Officer Deckard cited one violent incident. He related a fight between three local white teens and three black youths "who had moved to Bloomington from Chicago where they had been affiliated with gangs." Officer Deckard arrested two of the black juveniles (one escaped), charging them with criminal recklessness and assault with a deadly weapon. However, [according to D. Denny,] "The case was eventually dropped when the white youths refused to press charges." Officer Deckard's account of a local violent event involved teens suspected of gang affiliation, or at least past gang affiliation, but did not result in a gang-related arrest. No one discussed the last key indicator outlined by the Indianapolis gang task force commander. Bloomington's criminal justice officials, influenced by outside colleagues, insisted Bloomington had a gang problem based primarily on anecdotal evidence rather than gang-motivated crime.

A Lack of Evidence

Similar to the face-to-face interactions described by [E.H.] Sutherland in his differential association theory of crime, face-to-face interactions with outside law enforcement provided Bloomington's criminal justice personnel with definitions favorable to perceiving gangs in Bloomington. As a result of learned definitions, Bloomington's police conjured up a sinister, urban-generated gang presence based on little direct evidence of gang-related crime. At the same time, the county sheriff's department reported gangs constituted only a minor problem rather than a looming presence. If gangs threatened Bloomington, arrests of gang members should have readily occurred. Instead, it took almost a year for a gang-related arrest to materialize.

By December 1992, Bloomington Police arrested and charged two members of the Third World Shotgun Crypts with felonies. Although Sergeant Mike Diekhoff said these arrests resulted from a long-term investigation of gangs and drug-dealing activity, the probable cause affidavit emphasized only the number of members and the gang's written description of "a 'beat-down' as an initiation ceremony."

As a result of the group's size ("a group with at least five members") and literature about initiation beat-downs ("the offense of battery"), the Third World Shotgun Crypts met Indiana's legal definition of a gang. Although in line with Indiana's gang statute, these gang arrests and convictions did not substantiate learned claims about migrating, drug-peddling gangsters. Indeed, these arrests provided little evidence of gang crime. By the time plea agreements were reached, even the officer who filed the probable cause affidavit said that Third World Shotgun Crypts members committed no serious crimes. The deputy public defender concluded, "Police have said organized gangs are trying to move in here. If that's true, this is not it." Even so, police suspicions of a gang threat produced a war on drugs that democratically sought out any user-powerful or powerless, white or black, affluent or poor. . . .

Arrests . . . did not produce the urban, drug-dealing gangsters predicted by outside police. With no urban gang members to arrest, Bloomington's police began arresting residents suspected of possessing marijuana. Police maintained that aggressive tactics and a zero tolerance towards drugs would deter an influx of drug-dealing gangsters. However, this police response to drugs fueled social unrest in the community. Residents protested about police conduct, gained supportive media attention, and denounced the police zero tolerance as inappropriate for their city. Most telling is the fact that no urban, drug-dealing gang members were arrested by Bloomington's police during the time period covered by this paper.

My findings suggest that urban police information about crime may be inappropriate for smaller contexts. Clearly, law enforcement ideas about urban gangs and the aggressive tactics necessary to fight drugs did not fit the small city context of Bloomington. My research upholds the Department of Justice warning against assuming crimes in smaller settings "are 'urban processes written small' at least without more empirical evidence to indicate it is reasonable to do this."

"Most gangs have members who are involved in drug trafficking."

Drug Trafficking by Gangs Is a Serious Problem

National Alliance of Gang Investigators Associations

In the following viewpoint the National Alliance of Gang Investigators Associations (NAGIA) claims that in a majority of U.S. communities reporting gang activity, drug trafficking is a significant part of gang culture. Drug sales, NAGIA maintains, are a way gang members make money and also a reason gangs and gang violence have begun to spread to other communities. Drug trafficking is so much a part of gang culture that it has changed the nature of gangs: Instead of battling over turf, gangs now fight over the drug trade, the alliance argues. NAGIA, an alliance of sixteen regional associations, promotes and coordinates national antigang strategies.

As you read, consider the following questions:
1. To what does NAGIA attribute gang growth across the United States?
2. What conclusion does NAGIA draw based on the knowledge that racially mixed gangs are growing?
3. According to NAGIA, how do drugs drive, bind, and reinforce gang culture?

National Alliance of Gang Investigators Associations, "Section II. The National Gang Threat: Gang Growth and Migration," *National Gang Threat Assessment*, February 2000. Copyright © 2000 by the National Alliance of Gang Investigators Associations. All rights reserved. Reproduced by permission.

In the absence of strong family and community support, gang values have replaced traditional ethics and standards. . . . Local government officials, law enforcement professionals, and community leaders from smaller cities once thought to be immune to the crime and violence associated with gangs have witnessed the emergence and growth of gangs.

They have gone so far as to identify the growth of gangs as an "epidemic." Much of the gang growth across the United States can be attributed to the influence of the gang subculture rather than actual gang migration. Many communities are experiencing gang emulation or localized imitations of nationally recognized gangs. Familiar gang names from Chicago and Los Angeles are appearing in cities across the country, with no apparent connection to these nationally known gangs.

The migration of gang members—not the entire gang—has also contributed to the growth of gangs. They migrate and form a new gang by recruiting members from the local area. The National Youth Gang Center reports that 89 percent of the respondents to its 1997 survey indicated that some gang members had migrated to their jurisdictions and estimated that 23 percent of their gang members were migrants. Small cities and rural counties reported that, on average, more than 36 percent of their gang members had migrated from other jurisdictions. Reports of big-city gang members dispersing across the nation seeking new markets for drug distribution have fueled concerns about gang migration. In communities where drug trafficking is their primary criminal activity, gangs battle for market share in the drug trade, rather than over turf as they did in the late 1980s and early 1990s. Gang migration from larger cities to smaller communities occurs for many reasons:

- Family relocations
- Moves in connection with training and rehabilitation programs
- Attempts to avoid apprehension and prosecution
- Attempts to avoid retribution from rival gang members
- The opening or expansion of drug markets for higher profits
- Less rivalry and competition

- An environment where it is easier to intimidate and manipulate the community
- Limited anti-gang resources and lack of gang recognition or awareness by law enforcement

A Universal Problem

When gangs were primarily an urban problem, each gang's members were usually of one racial or ethnic group. As gangs migrated into the suburbs and rural areas, they began to recruit members from various racial and ethnic groups. Gangs today are increasingly multicultural, multiracial, and multiethnic. According to Detective Wes Daily, Jr., President of the East Coast Gang Investigators Association, "It used to be young African-American males were the ones with their pants dropped below their waistlines, shoes untied, and hats flipped to the side. Today, street gangsters share this style and trend with the white youth of America. Culturally and racially mixed gangs are growing. Teachers, law enforcement professionals, parents, businesses, and corporations need to be educated on the subject. This is no longer about 'them,' it is about all of 'us.'" . . .

While part of the apparent growth is the result of a lessening of gang denial, experts agree that there has been a substantial growth in the number of gangs and gang members over the past two decades. The trend revealed from various studies is disturbing.

The most recent estimates reveal that more than 2,900 cities and towns with populations under 25,000 have active gangs. Gangs in these smaller jurisdictions place a great burden on community and law enforcement resources. . . .

The Drug-Gang Connection

Most gangs have members who are involved in drug trafficking to some extent. However, the level of drug trafficking by gang members varies regionally. According to respondents to the National Youth Gang Center's 1997 survey, it is estimated that 42 percent of gangs were involved in the street sale of drugs and 33 percent were involved in drug distribution for the specific purpose of generating profits for the gang. More than 90 percent of the jurisdictions reporting gang activity in the *National Drug Intelligence Center (NDIC) National Street Gang Survey Report—1998* stated that their gangs were involved in local drug sales, while 47 percent reported gang involvement in interstate drug trafficking.

Common Differences Between Street Gangs and Drug Gangs

Street Gangs	Drug Gangs
Versatile ("cafeteria-style") crime	Crime focused on drug business
Larger structures	Smaller structures
Less cohesive	More cohesive
Looser leadership	More centralized leadership
Ill-defined roles	Market-defined roles
Code of loyalty	Requirement of loyalty
Residential territories	Sales market territories
Members may sell drugs	Members do sell drugs
Intergang rivalries	Competition controlled
Younger on average, but wider age range	Older on average, but narrower age range

Malcolm W. Klein, *The American Street Gang*. New York: Oxford University Press, 1995.

Gang involvement in drug trafficking ranges from street-level sales to wholesale distribution. The typical scenario of gang participation in drug trafficking involves the entrepreneurial gang member who shifts a retail drug trafficking operation into an adjoining community or state. This move could be either temporary or long-term. On the other hand, the Black Gangster Disciples exemplify an organized interstate drug trafficking gang that has extended its network to over 40 states. In 1997, seven leaders of the gang were convicted of a drug conspiracy that the U.S. Attorney alleged took in over $100 million a year in cocaine and heroin sales. Numerous law enforcement agencies report that some gangs involved in wholesale drug distribution have connections to major international drug trafficking organizations.

Drug trafficking by gangs primarily involves cocaine and marijuana. However, gangs in California, the upper Midwest, and New England are increasingly involved in heroin trafficking. Methamphetamine trafficking by gangs is common in the western half of the United States and appears to follow the eastward migration of Hispanic gangs. Drug trafficking drives, binds, and reinforces gang culture by the criminal activity itself, as well as providing lucrative profits for the gang and individual gang members. Major aspects of gangs and drugs are best illustrated through responses provided for the *NDIC National Street Gang Survey Report—1998*. The following summaries are from survey responses:

Drug Trafficking Is a Key Economic Crime for Gangs
- The moneymaker for our gang members is the sale of drugs. Most of our crime is a spin-off of the drug business (St. Paul, Minnesota, Police Department).
- Narcotics sales have become the gangs' number-one activity because of the amount of money that can be made (Chicago, Illinois, Police Department).

Drugs Contribute to Gang Violence
- Most of the violent crimes involving these gangs are the results of their drug trafficking (Phoenix, Arizona, Police Department).
- Gangs are heavily tied into our drug trade and it is well known that drugs also greatly influence the crime rate and crime in general. We've had an increase in gang-related shootings in 1997 (Akron, Ohio, Police Department).

Drugs Influence Gang Migration
- We are currently experiencing migration from different cities in California. The reason for this migration is narcotics-related. Instances where new subjects come in and set up narcotics activity are on the rise. We are also seeing an influx of gang members from both Oklahoma City, Oklahoma, and Wichita Falls, Texas. Gang members involved in narcotics are about 50 percent of the narcotics problem, with the vast majority being involved in the trafficking of crack cocaine (Lawton, Oklahoma, Police Department).
- Rolling 60s members have contacts in California, Oregon, Washington, and now Montana. These individuals are into narcotics (interstate and local), money launder-

ing, and weapons violations (Great Falls, Montana, Police Department).

Drugs Cause Gangs to Change Their Criminal Culture and Tactics

- In some cases, the Bloods and Crips have joined forces to sell crack cocaine. They are overlooking the red and blue in their pursuit of money. This trend is most noticeable in older gang members (Portland, Oregon, Police Bureau).
- A recent trend in the Arlington Heights area is the aligning of Folk and People gangs with each other for the benefit of narcotics trafficking (Arlington Heights, Illinois, Police Department).

"Urban-style gangs have been springing up on Indian reservations across the country."

Gangs in Native American Communities Are a Growing Problem

Vince Beiser

The problem of gang violence is threatening Native American communities as the gang influence spreads across reservations nationwide, argues Vince Beiser in the following viewpoint. The murder rate on reservations began to rise at the same time gangs arrived, he claims. Unlike their urban counterparts, Beiser maintains, Native American gangs are motivated by prestige, not money. Beiser, who writes on criminal justice issues, is senior editor at *Mother Jones*'s online publication, *MoJo Wire*.

As you read, consider the following questions:

1. In Beiser's view, what is the difference between the high-desert hinterland of the Navajos' southwestern reservation and its capital, Window Rock?
2. According to Beiser, why are Indian reservations fertile ground for criminal gangs?
3. In the author's opinion, how are young Indians bringing gang culture to the reservation?

Vince Beiser, "Boys on the Rez—Window Rock Dispatch," *The New Republic*, July 10, 2000, p. 15. Copyright © 2000 by The New Republic, Inc. Reproduced by permission of *The New Republic*.

Randy, a stocky, dark-skinned 28-year-old, sits on a folding chair in the dirt yard outside his battered one-story house. Dressed in baggy jeans and a black hooded sweatshirt, he recounts how his gang, the Insane Cobra Nation, took over the rundown housing projects he's lived in since he was nine. "At first it was just about beating people up for money," Randy says. "Then it built up to where people started shooting at us, and us at them." Not long ago, he boasts, pointing down the road to a spot just past an abandoned house slathered with gang tags, his Cobras stabbed a former comrade-in-arms 13 times for joining the rival West Siders. "I grew up in a fucked-up household," Randy says by way of explaining how he joined his gang. "My dad was an alcoholic. . . . I grew up poor. . . . The only people who would help me out were my bros, the Cobras. They became my family."

A New Gang Landscape

Randy's trajectory—from childhood poverty to adult gang violence—is so familiar that it's practically become a cliche of inner-city life. But Randy's story has a twist: From where he's sitting in his front yard, there's no major city for hundreds of miles. Despite his homeboy outfit and affect, the "streets" his gang claims are mostly dirt roads.

Randy Wauneka is a full-blooded Navajo Indian, and the Insane Cobra Nation's turf is on the Navajos' Southwestern reservation, 25,000 square miles of dry scrubland and soaring red-rock spires. Out in the reservation's high-desert hinterland, tribal elders still herd sheep and sleep in traditional hogans. But in the reservation's capital, Window Rock, a cheerless sprawl of low stucco houses and trailer homes, tags from the Navajo Nation's 50 gangs mark every bridge and street sign.

And it's not just Window Rock: urban-style gangs have been springing up on Indian reservations across the country. [In 1994] according to the Bureau of Indian Affairs (BIA), there were 181 known Indian gangs. [As of July 2000], the BIA estimates, there are some 520, with a total of more than 6,000 members—from the Bitches for Life among South Dakota's Rosebud tribe to the Red Pride Bloods on Arizona's Tohono O'Odham reservation.

The effect of gangs on Indian communities has been profound. While some gangs are relatively harmless—consisting of packs of alienated Indian youths doing nothing more serious than spray-painting walls—others aren't so benign. In recent years, Window Rock's murder rate has surged past Chicago's and Los Angeles's; at one point, the homicide rate on Montana's Fort Peck reservation was more than double the rate in New Orleans. Indeed, while the nationwide homicide rate has fallen steadily in the last decade—dropping 37 percent between 1992 and 1998, the most recent year for which complete statistics are available—reported murders on Indian reservations shot up by 50 percent between 1992 and 1999. A . . . federal study found that American Indians are now twice as likely to be victims of violent crime as members of any other ethnic or racial group. Says Gordon Toadlena, supervisor of the Navajo police department's Window Rock criminal-investigations unit, "The murders went up when we started having gang problems."

A Fertile Ground

Long plagued by poverty, alcohol abuse, family dysfunction, and the anger of the marginalized, Indian reservations are fertile ground for criminal gangs. The demographics don't help either: the median age of American Indians is 24, as opposed to 33 for other Americans. On many reservations, half the population is under 18.

That Indian gangs copy the culture of their urban counterparts is little wonder. After all, mainstream American society is seeping onto reservations like never before. Thanks to MTV, CDs, and the Internet, some young Indians know more about Snoop Dogg's history than about the history of their people. "I don't know what Navajo culture really is," says a rail-thin young Navajo who calls himself Xpres and performs with the Window Rock rap group Tribal Live, "so I can't say I take part in it."

And it's not just technology that's bringing gang culture to reservations; young Indians are bringing it themselves. Increasing numbers of Native Americans are spending time in big cities, where many get involved in gang life and bring it back when they return home. The Cobras, for instance, were

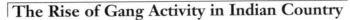

The Rise of Gang Activity in Indian Country

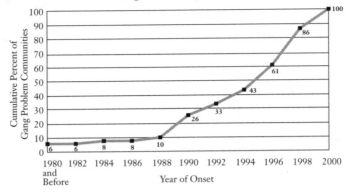

Aline K. Major and Arlen Egley Jr., *OJJDP: NYGC Fact Sheet*, June 2002.

started by a Navajo who moved to Chicago, joined a gang, and then returned to Window Rock. Many Indians also join gangs in state and federal prisons, which currently house more than 12,000 Indians—a number that has doubled since 1990.

The Turf Warriors

But, while Indian gangs copy the styles of their urban counterparts, they may surpass them when it comes to the senselessness of their violence. On reservations, commercial crimes—like drug deals, robberies, and carjackings—aren't a major source of intergang violence. Instead, it consists mostly of gang members attacking each other, either to gain prestige or out of simple malice. "They're not into gangs for the money," says William Mitchell Jr., a BIA police officer who until recently patrolled several reservations near Albuquerque, New Mexico. "It's more about the glamour and trying to be the tough guy." Says Joe Lodge, a prosecutor with the U.S. attorney's office in Phoenix, "The violence is real turf-oriented. It's 'You're in our area wearing the wrong color or flashing the wrong signs, so we're gonna get you, because that's what we see on TV.'"

The turf wars can be particularly brutal. In 1996, when the Cobras took on a rival gang called the Dragons, murders on the Navajo reservation hit a record 67. "There were drive-bys every weekend," recalls Sergeant Wallace Billie, a thickset Navajo police officer. "We had lots of bodies popping up." Even the little Salt River Pima-Maricopa reservation near Phoenix saw dozens of drive-by shootings, which culminated in 1997 when five members of its East Side Crips Rolling Thirties gang were sent to prison on charges ranging from murder to witness intimidation.

An Ill-Equipped Police Force

Yet, for all this urban-style mayhem, reservation police forces remain staffed and equipped at sub-Podunk levels: While the average small town has 2.9 cops per 1,000 residents, the average reservation has only 1.3. Making matters worse, tribal police often have to cover huge swatches of territory, with no backup officers for miles. [In December 1999] a police officer arriving alone at the scene of a reported break-in on Arizona's White River Apache reservation was shot to death; he was the only officer on duty at that time on the entire reservation. And, even when the cops do arrest people, dilapidated jails barely hold them. Half a dozen prisoners escaped from the Window Rock Tribal Jail one recent year before police discovered that the back door could be opened with a piece of wire.

In response, many reservations have shifted their strained resources to the fight against youth crime; as of 1998, 15 tribes had created gang task forces. And this year the Navajo Nation began work on the first youth correctional facility on an Indian reservation. What's more, the federal government—responsible for most of the public security in what is called "Indian country—has belatedly boosted law enforcement funding . . . partly in response to the gang problem. [In 2000], the Clinton administration . . . asked Congress for an extra $103 million for Indian law enforcement. Those infusions have swelled the BIA's law enforcement budget by more than $20 million in each of the last two years.

But it's not nearly enough. "When you spread that out across the whole country, it doesn't go a long way," says Mike McCoy, BIA district commander for the New Mexico area. "It means an extra car here, some extra body armor there." Things have calmed down a bit on the Navajo reser-

59

vation . . . since an FBI-led crackdown landed 14 top Cobras in prison. [The 1999] murder rate was the lowest in five years. But no one thinks the gangs are gone for good. Indeed, on the last day of 1999, four Cobras broke into a house and stole a collection of sniper rifles and a .45 pistol. With 300 Cobras still active, not to mention rivals like the Killer Park Crips and West Siders, it's only a matter of time before trouble flares up again. "We don't have the capacity to either suppress or rehabilitate these guys," says Stewart Calnimptewa, a Navajo former cop who now runs a security firm specializing in gang trouble. "We'll see a surge in crime again. The boys are getting restless."

Randy Wauneka agrees. "Once in a gang, you're down for life," he says. "I couldn't just say, 'I want out.' All the respect I've got now, I'd be throwing it down the shithole. And then my old homies would start punkin' me. I was born a Navajo and I'll always be a Navajo. But I'll be a gang member, too, till the day I die."

> *"Female gang membership has continued to increase as lawmakers, law-enforcement officials and community groups scramble to resist this bizarre phenomenon."*

The Number of Girl Gang Members Is Growing

Catherine Edwards

In the following viewpoint Catherine Edwards claims that girl gang members are rising in number, and their role within gangs is changing. Once cheerleaders for male gang members, girls are now considered full gang members. Female gang members arouse less suspicion than their male counterparts when conducting illegal gang activities and are more likely to hold down responsible jobs, Edwards maintains. Girl gang members are also exceedingly violent, argues Edwards, often slashing the faces of rival gang members with razor blades. Edwards is a staff writer for *Insight on the News* magazine.

As you read, consider the following questions:
1. What did the FBI's Uniform Crime Reports reveal about female juvenile crime?
2. According to Edwards, what is the difference between girls who "jump in" or "sex in" to become gang members?
3. Why do some teenage mothers join gangs, in the author's view?

Catherine Edwards, "When Girl Power Goes Gangsta," *Insight on the News*, March 20, 2000. Copyright © 2000 by News World Communications, Inc. All rights reserved. Reproduced by permission.

S hermika Booker is a different person today than she was two years ago. She smiles, talks about how glad she is that she finished high school and says she hopes someday to become a dental assistant. But things were not so rosy in 1998.

Booker, 20, and a group of other girls who also live in the Garfield neighborhood in upper Northwest Washington [D.C.]—just two miles from the White House—had a "beef," or fight, with the girls of a nearby housing development called Park Moreton. The Garfield girls dubbed themselves the "Shank 'Em Up Honeys"; their enemies at Park Moreton were the "No Limit Honeys." Rivalry escalated to violence and the girls fought with knives, or shanks, and guns.

A Surprising New Phenomenon

Teen-age girls trying to kill each other? None who watched the rival Sharks and Jets meet for a "rumble" in *West Side Story* would recognize gangs today. These days, authorities are learning to keep their eyes open for middle-school girls and their high-school mentors who play as rough—or rougher—as the boys. "It's like gender liberation has hit the gangs," John Anderson, deputy district attorney for Orange County, Calif., told the *Orange County Register* in the early 1990s. "Girl gangsters aren't going to knock you down; they're going to make you hurt and make it last." And that was then. Female gang membership has continued to increase as lawmakers, law-enforcement officials and community groups scramble to resist this bizarre phenomenon.

In 1991 a group of eight men, all friends and native Washingtonians, met in the hair salon of Tyrone Parker, now president of the Alliance of Concerned Men, an organization that brokered the truce that eventually ended the fighting between rival toughs. Concerned that the neighborhoods of the nation's capital had become much more dangerous than when they grew up, they decided to start meeting with the most violent kids in the city. Nine years later, the men have helped establish positive programs for young people all over Washington [D.C.].

When fighting broke out among individual girls in the rival neighborhoods of Northwest Washington, their parents—for whatever reason—were not involved in the lives of their kids, and many of the girls organized for protection, says Mack Alsobrooks of the Alliance. "They started dropping out of school and arming themselves. Some of the girls became prisoners in their own homes," he explains.

"If it wasn't for the Alliance, I'd still be on the streets," Booker tells *Insight*. But most teen-age girls who become involved in neighborhood violence and gang warfare are not so lucky. "We are predisposed to male gang members with our mentoring programs. Everything we do for males we now need to do for females," says Det. Sgt. Scott Lawson of the Polk County Sheriff's Department in Florida. He helped start the gang unit in the Lakeland region in 1995. "They are no longer second-class gangs. We cannot ignore them. They are selling drugs and doing drive-by shootings."

Lawson tells of his surprise at investigating a crime spree by a group in his county called the Gangster Disciples. The 10 gang members had committed armed robbery, assault, burglary and a shooting. "While this may seem run-of-the mill gang crime, what got our attention was that eight of the 10 members were females and a female was calling the shots for this particular outing," he says.

A Change in Female Juvenile Crime

The numbers of incarcerated women have tripled since the late 1980s, according to the FBI's Uniform Crime Reports. While violent-crime rates are decreasing nationally, female juvenile crime is on the increase. Total crime arrests of female juveniles increased 118 percent between 1987 and 1996. In 1989, eight males were arrested for every female. At the close of the last decade, that ratio was down to 5-to-1. The percentage of female gang involvement nationally is estimated at 10 to 15 percent; their ages range from 9 to 24.

"They are not doing typical female crimes anymore either, like prostitution," says Sandra Hahn of the Washington County, Minn., Department of Court Services. "They are committing violent as well as white-collar crime, computer-chip theft, phone cloning, ATM cash-card cloning. They are smart. Because they might not be as strong as males they use weapons like knives and razor blades and go for the face in a fight."

Hahn says she is concerned whether officers are properly trained in handling girl gangsters, and she travels nationally to train and educate authorities about how to deal with female offenders. She started monitoring girls in gangs through "ride-alongs" into gang territory with the Los Angeles Police Department when California was almost alone in tracking female gang involvement. She found that there was not a great deal of information on girls in gangs and that many in law enforcement as recently as the mid-1990s never had considered that females could be as violent—let alone more dangerous—than males.

"The girls used to be the cheerleaders for their gang-member boyfriends and actually served as deterrents for crimes because the boys wanted to protect them," notes Mike Knox, formerly with the Houston Police Department and author of *Gangsta in the House*. "The big trend now is for girls to form their own gangs, and some are in competition with the male gangs. Young women are realizing they can engage in all manner of crime like men."

The Power of Girl Gang Members

The Chicago Crime Commission, a nonprofit organization dedicated to improving public safety in the greater Chicago area, issued a study on girls in gangs in 1999. It found that girl gangsters tended to fall into four categories: auxiliary members of male gangs, female members of co-ed gangs, female leaders within co-ed gangs and all-female gangs. The female members wear the gang colors with as much pride as their male counterparts. They even feminize their gang names. Instead of Latin Kings, they call themselves the Latin Queens. They are not just Gangster Disciples but Lady Disciplettes. Girls are organized in white-supremacist gangs, Asian gangs, Pakistani gangs, African-American gangs and Latino and Latina gangs.

According to George Knox, editor of the *Journal of Gang Research* at the National Gang Crime Research Center in Chicago, initiation for female gang members is as harsh as for the males. Girls either go through a "jump in," which may require a violent beating from gang members, or a "sex in." But girls who are initiated into the gang by a "sex in" usually do not command the same respect as those "jumped in" and are less likely to rise in the ranks, says Knox. He notes how shocked the public was about a case in Texas in which two teen-age girls were required to have sex with HIV-positive gang members as part of the initiation ceremony.

Female Gang Members Grow More Violent

An 11-city survey of eighth graders undertaken in the mid-1990's found that more than 90 percent of both male and female gang members reported having engaged in one or more violent acts in the previous 12 months. The researchers found that 78 percent of female gang members reported being involved in gang fights, 65 percent reported carrying a weapon for protection, and 39 percent reported attacking someone with a weapon. These and similar findings prompted the authors of this study to recommend that gang prevention and intervention efforts be directed specifically at females.

Joan Moore and John Hagedorn, *Juvenile Justice Bulletin*, March 2001.

Many male gang members sport elaborate tattoos denoting their affiliation. The girls also are tattooed. Detectives say that if girls are part of a male gang, they often are asked to commit crimes at the gang leader's bidding. In addition, many law-enforcement officers interviewed by *Insight* conceded that girls are able to get away with more criminal activity. "Cops are less suspicious of a girl driving by with a baby in the back seat," says Mike Knox.

Some females are lured into gangs by the promise of financial reward, identity and status, according to Kristen Lindberg, author of the Chicago Crime Commission report on girl gangsters. Lindberg also notes that females are more likely to hold down a respectable job at the same time that they are involved in gang activity, also making them look less suspicious. Some of the police officers with whom Lindberg spoke said they seldom question the girls at crime scenes.

Why Girls Join Gangs

Females seem to put up with a great deal of mistreatment by their gang leaders. "I found that many of the girls had come from extremely exploitive and abusive backgrounds," says Hahn. "When the gang leaders treated them poorly, they thought this was normal behavior." Teen-age mothers often join gangs to provide a surrogate family for their children. "We now have 25-year-old grandmothers in gangs," reports Mike Knox. Other girl gangsters don't want to be subject to the authority of the boys. They join girl gangs because they have become tired of being the ones committing the crimes, running the drugs and putting themselves in danger, says Hahn.

Others from more traditional ethnic backgrounds want to form their own gangs to break out of inherited second-class-citizen roles that their mothers play. "Things that happen around the world affect us here in law enforcement," explains Bruce Wiley, a detective with the gang unit in Fairfax County, Va. "When Vietnam fell, refugees flooded to the U.S.; the same with the strife in El Salvador. A small number of these immigrants began taking advantage of the system and forming gangs."

Westminster, Calif., a town of 80,000 that lies 40 miles west of Los Angeles, has the largest Vietnamese business district in the free world. Sgt. Marcus Franks, a detective and gang investigator with the organized-crime unit there, tells *Insight*, "This is the center of Vietnamese gangs in the United States." His team has counted seven all-female Southeast Asian gangs in the area.

The first Vietnamese girl gangsters had come straight from the refugee camps, says Franks, so life in the United States was frightening but liberating. Teaming up with their male friends in gangs provided financial and social security that these girls never had experienced. But more than 25 years have passed since the end of the Vietnam War, and the first generation of American-born Vietnamese is doing its own thing. "They never had the refugee-camp experience," says Franks. "They see Occidental gangs in the media and want to pattern themselves after them. They are seriously engaged in organized crime, and some aspire to be an Asian John Gotti."

Franks notes that the girls have incredibly low self-esteem because they have rejected their ethnic culture but are not fully embraced by the male gangs because they are in competition with them. "This makes them work to be more tough and ultimately as dangerous," he says.

Wiley monitors Vietnamese gangs in Northern Virginia and recently worked a case in which a group of girl gangsters beat a 14-year-old girl within an inch of her life. "She said the wrong thing about a rival gang and they made her pay for it," he tells *Insight*.

The Problem of Denial

Denial is the biggest problem among parents, educators, law enforcement, community and church groups, says Wiley. "No one wants to admit that their little girl could be involved in a gang. I spend a great deal of time going around talking about gang problems and educating people and police academies about what to look for. Parents must be involved in their kids' lives if we are going to curb gang growth," he says.

There is no law against being in a gang. Most are efficiently run and leaders command absolute authority. One of the most well-known gang leaders is Larry Hoover. He runs the Gangster Disciples from prison in Illinois, where he is serving a sentence of 200 years. The gang even has a Website. Gang members tend to thrive in prison, where gangs are very powerful, says Mike Knox.

Many juvenile offenders are sent to "boot camp," a punishment meant to reform wayward youth. Boot camps have been a topic of controversy as lawmakers debate their effectiveness in fighting crime. "We are training our juvenile gang members by sending them to boot camp," Wiley complains. "They come out tougher and stronger, ready more than ever for gang warfare."

"Kids don't need boot-camp foolishness, and they can be controlled without gun control and TV control. You've got to control their hearts," insists Robert Woodson, president of the National Center for Neighborhood Enterprise, a Washington-based organization dedicated to assisting low-income, self-help groups nationwide. Woodson acknowledges that girl gangs often go unnoticed and are a growing problem in many communities. He advocates intervention on a local level and supports the work of the Alliance of Concerned Men.

Alsobrooks of the Alliance of Concerned Men says that the warring Washington neighborhoods of Garfield and Park Moreton have been violence-free for two years because the girls realized that the enemies they were stabbing and shooting were a lot like themselves. He acknowledges that girls, in particular, need encouragement and self-esteem. "We give out a lot of hugs," he says.

"We are all friends now," Booker tells *Insight*. Alsobrooks smiles, and says, "Yes, our ladies are magnificent."

"[U.S.] Gang 'franchises' have taken hold in El Salvador, Honduras and Guatemala."

Deported U.S. Gang Members Threaten Central American Communities

Rupert Widdicombe and Duncan Campbell

In the following viewpoint Rupert Widdicombe and Duncan Campbell, foreign correspondents for the *Guardian International*, argue that U.S. immigration reform that requires the deportation of convicted gang members, once refugees, has spread violent gang culture to Central America. Officials in El Salvador, the authors maintain, believe gang members are responsible for 10 percent of the annual murder rate. In addition to violence, the authors claim, deported gang members bring criminal sophistication to Central American gangs.

As you read, consider the following questions:

1. According to the authors, what initially motivated refugees to form gangs?
2. In the authors' view, what is unique about the Mara Salvatrucha gang compared to U.S. street gangs?
3. What has been the official response to gangs in Central America, in the authors' opinion?

Rupert Widdicombe and Duncan Campbell, "Poor Neighbours Fall Prey to US Gang Culture," *The Guardian*, March 27, 2003. Copyright © 2003 by Guardian Publications, Ltd. Reproduced by permission of Guardian News Service, Ltd.

The signs of the influence of the United States on Central America are everywhere: McDonald's and KFC, movies and sportswear. Less easy to spot is one export which has a devastating effect on the region: gang culture.

[In 1996], the Illegal Immigration Reform and Immigrant Responsibility Act was introduced in the US, which allowed the "expedited removal" of immigrants who had committed crimes.

This has led to the deportations to Central America of thousands of gang members, mainly from the Los Angeles region, who arrived in the US as children with their parents. Back in Central America they are retaining their structures. Gang "franchises" have taken hold in El Salvador, Honduras and Guatemala.

Exporting Violent Crime

The influence of US gang culture is evident in poor neighbourhoods or barrios across Central America. There are local variations on a dress code of baggy clothes, baseball caps and chains, a defined taste in music (much of it Latino rap and hip-hop), a semiology in tattoos, graffiti and hand signs, and a slang peppered with imported words like broderes (brothers) and "homies". Most damaging is a fashion for extreme violence that has found an easy home in countries with violent histories.

In El Salvador, with a population of 6 million, a survey put gang membership at 20,000. Gang members are thought to be responsible for 10% of El Salvador's annual murder rate of 120 killings for every 100,000 people. The economic impact is huge: a study commissioned by the Inter-American Development Bank found that 12% of GNP is spent on dealing with violence and its consequences.

In Guatemala, with a population of 13 million, the police calculate that there are more than 300 gangs with a total membership of 200,000. In Honduras, with a population of 6 million, there are said to be 60,000 gang members.

The two major international "franchises" are the MS (Mara Salvatrucha) and the Mara 18 (also known as MS-18 and Calle 18). Local branches of these gangs are involved in major crime from smuggling drugs and weapons, to kidnapping and car-jacking.

A Truly International Gang

The spread of the gangs has its origins in the conflicts that have racked Central America during the past 25 years. In the early 1980s, more than 1 million refugees fled to the US during El Salvador's civil war, which killed 75,000 people.

Some had ties with La Mara, a street gang from the capital, San Salvador. Others had been members of groups such as the leftwing Farabundo Marti National Liberation front. Many settled in Los Angeles and found themselves in conflict with local Latino gangs.

Al Valdez, a district attorney investigator for Orange County in California specialising in gangs, said initially the gangs had been formed for self-protection, but "quickly developed a reputation for being organised and extremely violent". According to Mr Valdez, Mara Salvatrucha has expanded across the US, Canada, and Mexico.

"MS is unique in that, unlike traditional US street gangs, it maintains active ties with MS members and factions in El Salvador. Mara Salvatrucha is truly an international gang."

The Tragic Consequences

Deportations to El Salvador began after the immigration act was passed and now about 300 arrive from the US every month. It is a similar story in Guatemala and Honduras, where the latest annual figures show that 8,000 have been deported from the US.

Miguel Cruz a Salvadorean academic and author said: "Only a few of the deportees are criminals, but they have a significant influence on the local gang members. They quickly become leaders and role models for the youngest."

Increased sophistication is one thing the deportees bring. Oscar Alavarez, Honduras minister of security, said a police raid on one gang . . . uncovered a book which detailed all their transactions, from the costs of transport to ammunition. "They communicate on the internet, they run the gangs like a business."

On April 5, [2003] 69 people were killed in El Porvenir prison in La Ceiba, Honduras, of whom 61 were members of Mara 18. Most were shot by guards. Many bodies had been burnt. President Ricardo Maduro has ordered an investigation but relatives claim most were killed after they surrendered.

Jorge Hernandez, Honduras minister of the interior, said the influence of the gangs now permeated the country's way of life. The government is spending $30m (£18m) a year on projects to take people out of the gangs but the gangs are growing.

A Typical Story of Poor Salvadoran Refugees

Wito's [Giovanni Castro's] story is typical of the thousands of Salvadoran gang members who learned the ropes on American city streets. They were refugees who fled right-wing violence in the 1980s or children of those refugees. While the wealthy packed their kids off to condos and private schools in Miami or San Francisco to wait out the war, children of the poor who stole across the border were often left with a single working parent or sometimes no parent at all, largely abandoned to the streets once they reached the States. They learned gang rites at a young age, inhabiting a world within our borders that is almost completely hidden from our view. As anti-immigrant sentiments reached a fever pitch in the mid-1990s, Congress broadened the range of criminal acts that could result in expulsion, producing a surge in deportations to El Salvador. Salvadoran jails are overflowing, and local authorities have no choice but to give the deportados a fresh chance once they return home, since they have no criminal record in El Salvador. Often speaking little Spanish and with few hopes of finding gainful employment, the deportees quickly find themselves immersed in a culture of drugs and gangs remarkably similar to the one they left behind in the States.

Scott Wallace, *Harper's Magazine*, August 2000.

The official response in Central America has been a mix of repression and attempts to open a dialogue with gangs and young people: about a third of the region's population are under 10. Half are under 20. In Nicaragua, the police set up "prevention committees" and began visiting gang members and their families.

The hope is to prevent MS and Mara 18 taking hold there. The organisation Ceprev has worked with more than 3,000 pandilleros (gang members) over the past six years in one district of Managua with the aim of improving their relations with their families. Its director, Monica Zalaquette, says: "The problem is not economic poverty, it is the poverty of our family culture—that's what we have to change."

Bruce Harris of Casa Alianza, which works with at-risk young people in Central America, said: "For years, the authorities have left young people without hope, without access to school or jobs and the only governmental response to youth dissent has been repression. We have forced the kids to the extremes of society and they have responded with violence. Gangs can no longer be ignored, especially if we want to live in peace."

Chained by Gang Life

Jose, 17, is chained by the ankle to an iron ring set into the floor of his parents' wooden shack. He spends his days in a chair, a few feet from a tiny black and white television. At night he is chained to the frame of his bed. He is freed only to perform what his mother calls "his bodily needs".

Jose is a member of Los Puenteros, a street gang from a poor neighbourhood in southern Managua, Nicaragua's capital. He is addicted to crack cocaine. To pay for it he breaks into people's houses or robs on the streets armed with a machete. He once took and sold his young cousins' school shoes and rucksacks. "I don't know how long we will keep him there," Dona Wilma, Jose's mother, said. Jose says nothing and doesn't take his eyes off the cartoons. "But what else can we do? If we didn't he would go out on the streets and be killed or arrested."

Without the chains, Jose would be on the run from the police with other members of Los Puenteros who were at a bar on May 17 when their leader, Tres Ojos (Three Eyes), killed a member of a rival gang with two machete blows to the head.

Inter-gang violence has increased to the point where an unofficial curfew operates in most of Managua's marginal neighbourhoods where more than 100 gangs operate.

In this city of 1.2 million people, police made more than 40,000 arrests of gang members in 2001.

Although the gang franchises have not spread to Nicaragua

because there have been relatively few deportations from the US, the Los Angeles culture has fuelled the growth of organised crime.

After dark, people close their doors and windows and the streets become a battleground between rival gangs armed with stones, machetes, pistols, and home-made mortars.

Nelly Rodriguez, a resident of the area known as Las Americas II, said: "When they start to fight, stones start flying in every direction. So many hit the roof of the house it feels like it is going to cave in and I get under the table with my children."

The risks to non-combatants are real. In March Yolanda Molina, 12, was shot dead in her home during a gunfight between rival gangs.

Periodical Bibliography

The following articles have been selected to supplement the diverse views presented in this chapter.

American Correctional Association — "Gangs Inside," *Corrections Compendium*, April 2000.

Terry Carter — "'Equality with a Vengeance': Violent Crimes and Gang Activity by Girls Skyrocket," *ABA Journal*, November 1999.

Kelly Creedon — "El Salvador: War on Gangs," *NACLA Report on the Americas*, November/December 2003.

Donna De Cesare — "Dangerous Exile: More than 400,000 Noncitizens Have Been Deported Since 1996 Because of Expanded Criminal Sentencing," *Colorlines*, Fall 2003.

Economist — "The Trouble with Gangs," January 16, 1999.

Economist — "Wild Things: Gangs," May 4, 2002.

James Emery — "Their World, Not Ours—Among Gangs in America," *World & I*, December 2002.

Jeff Glasser — "The Software Sopranos," *U.S. News & World Report*, February 7, 2000.

James C. Howell, Arlen Egley Jr., and Debra K. Gleason — "Modern Day Youth Gangs," *Juvenile Justice Bulletin*, June 2002.

James C. Howell and Debra K. Gleason — "Youth Gang Drug Trafficking," *Juvenile Justice Bulletin*, December 1999.

Issues & Controversies — "Teen Gangs," May 12, 2000.

Marcy Levin-Epstein, ed. — "Rise in Gang Activity Suspected," *Inside School Safety*, January 2004.

John McCormick — "Winning a Gang War," *Newsweek*, November 1, 1999.

Sarah McNaught — "Gansta Girls," *Boston Phoenix*, May 20–27, 1999.

Kit R. Roane, Angie Cannon, and Mike Tharp — "Deadly Numbers: Cops Fear New Surge," *U.S. News & World Report*, February 26, 2001.

David Starbuck, James C. Howell, and Donna J. Lindquist — "Hybrid and Other Modern Gangs," *Juvenile Justice Bulletin*, December 2001.

Mark Totten — "Dispelling Myths About Youth Violence," *Ottawa Citizen*, February 10, 1999.

Daniel B. Wood — "As Gangs Rise, So Do Calls for U.S.-Wide Dragnet," *Christian Science Monitor*, February 4, 2004.

CHAPTER 2

What Factors Encourage Gang Behavior?

Chapter Preface

In the decades since pioneering sociologist Frederick Thrasher came out in 1927 with *The Gang*, the first systematic study of gangs conducted in the United States, social scientists have written numerous books and articles examining the social factors, such as poverty and peer pressure, that cause young people to join and form gangs. However, much of this gang literature has focused exclusively on males. Researchers saw gangs as a quintessentially male phenomenon and tended to dismiss female gangs as satellites of male groups, and viewed female gang members as sex objects or tomboys. Criminologists Joan Moore and John Hagedorn note that the first book to treat female gangs in a serious fashion is Anne Campbell's *The Girls in the Gang*, published in 1984. Since then, a growing number of researchers have focused on the phenomenon of female gangs. Among the questions these researchers have sought to answer is whether boys and girls join or form gangs for the same reasons.

Many observers, such as gang investigator Marco Silva, argue that "girls join gangs for the same reasons boys do. . . . They want to belong to something, to be part of something because they lack respect from their homes." Other reasons cited by researchers for joining or remaining in gangs include the desire for prestige or status among one's peers, a chance for excitement, the lure of making money selling drugs, the influence of relatives who became gang members, or because youths feel threatened or pressured to join a gang to protect themselves from other gangs. Many researchers cite poverty, which limits both job and recreational opportunities for young people, as a major cause of both male and female gang involvement.

But some research has indicated that girl gang members have unique motivations for joining gangs. Many researchers have found a strong correlation between family sexual abuse and gang involvement, and have argued that gangs may, especially for girls, serve as a refuge from physical abuse at home. "There is evidence from several studies that, on the whole, girls come from more troubled families than boys," argues Meda Chesney-Lind and John Hagedorn, sociologists and editors of the book *Female Gangs in America*. "The female gang acts as a kind of a refuge for many girls, while for most boys the male gang is an extension of a mainstream, aggressive, male role."

How girls' and boys' experiences affect their decisions to join gangs is central to the study of how and why gangs form. The viewpoints in this chapter examine several risk factors that may cause youth of both sexes to join gangs.

"Through the marginalization and street socialization of urban youth and the creation of a street gang subculture, . . . the street gang becomes a subsociety."

Young People Join Gangs Because of Social Marginalization

James Diego Vigil

James Diego Vigil is a professor in the Department of Criminology, Law, and Society, at the University of California at Irvine, and the former director of the Center for the Study of Urban Poverty at the University of California at Los Angeles. His writings include the books *Barrio Gangs: Street Life and Identity in Southern California* and *A Rainbow of Gangs: Street Cultures in the Mega-City*, from which the following viewpoint is excerpted. In it he argues that street gangs are the outcome of a society in which members of impoverished ethnic groups and immigrant communities are marginalized by American society. He claims that young people, faced with weakened family ties, public schools that do not serve them, and little opportunities for legal employment, resort to creating their own welcoming communities through gangs.

As you read, consider the following questions:
1. What role does ethnicity play in gang formation, according to Vigil?
2. What voids in young people's lives are filled by "street socialization," according to the author?

James Diego Vigil, *A Rainbow of Gangs: Street Cultures in the Mega-City*. Austin: University of Texas Press, 2002. Copyright © 2002 by the University of Texas. All rights reserved. Reproduced by permission.

It is unavoidably clear that gangs constitute one of the most important urban youth issues in the United States today. Recent estimates place the number of gangs nationwide at 30,533 and the number of gang members at 815,896. The Los Angeles area tops the list with close to 8,000 gangs and 200,000 gang members. These figures are for males only; female gang members are many fewer in number (from 4 to 10 percent of all Los Angeles gang members), but their significance is considerable, for studies show that nationwide a high percentage of all incarcerated females belong to gangs. Furthermore, the arrest rates of young women recently have increased at a faster pace than for nongang males, and the types of offenses committed by them are becoming more serious and violent.

Since the early 1980s, drug trafficking and abuse, gang violence (often tied to drugs), and all sorts of other criminal activities have increased markedly across the United States. In Los Angeles County, gang homicides have recently gone down, but in the 1982–1991 period they climbed from 205 to 700, and by the middle of the 1990s they nearly topped 1,000. As U.S. society attempted to keep up with the crime problem during that period, the prison population tripled. In Los Angeles, the use of gang injunctions, battering rams, specialized gang law-enforcement units, and harsher penalties such as "three strikes" attest to a pervasive law and order preoccupation in dealing with youth in minority areas.

Street gangs do emerge primarily in low-income ethnic minority neighborhoods. Some of the Los Angeles gangs can be traced as far back as the 1930s. Initially no more than small bands of wayward children in East Los Angeles Chicano communities, these "boy gangs" metamorphosed over the decades into a deeply rooted gang subculture characterized by a collection of gangs fashioned within the communities of various ethnic groups. Social neglect, ostracism, economic marginalization, and cultural repression were largely responsible for the endurance of the subculture. When the economic structure of the city changed and large-scale immigration swept into the city from the 1960s forward, gang formation accelerated. No ethnic community has been immune to the problem, although the Chicano, African American, Vietnamese, and Central American communities have been especially affected. . . .

Ethnicity plays an important role when cultural groups live in close contact and their physical or cultural characteristics are used to create social boundaries. In Los Angeles, as elsewhere in the United States, ethnic minorities whose physical characteristics most clearly distinguish them from the white majority are most readily subjected to prejudice and discrimination. . . .

An Outcome of Marginalization

Basically, the street gang is an outcome of marginalization, that is, the relegation of certain persons or groups to the fringes of society, where social and economic conditions result in powerlessness. This process occurs on multiple levels as a product of pressures and forces in play over a long period of time. The phrase "multiple marginality" reflects the complexities and persistence of these forces. Macrohistorical and macrostructural forces—those that occur at the broader levels of society—lead to economic insecurity and lack of opportunity, fragmented institutions of social control, poverty, and psychological and emotional barriers among large segments of the ethnic minority communities in Los Angeles. These are communities whose members face inadequate living conditions, stressful personal and family changes, and racism and cultural repression in schools. . . .

Consider the pressures and strains in the lives of females, which are especially pronounced. They must contend with major forces from without and from within their own ethnic group and social class that deepen their experiencing of marginalization: exacerbated sexism (such as male dominance and exploitation), family friction related to the conflict between traditional cultural attitudes toward females and those of the general society, barriers to achieving economic well-being, and childbearing and childcare burdens. For them the marginalization processes are doubly compounded, since the protection and supervision traditionally afforded girls in a family's country of origin is lessened and they frequently become vulnerable to physical and sexual abuse and exploitation, often within their own families.

Daily strains from many directions take their toll and strip minority peoples of their coping skills. Being left out of mainstream society in so many ways and in so many places relegates these urban youths to the margins of society in practically every sense. This positioning leaves them with few options or resources to better their lives. Often, they seek a place where they are not marginalized—and find it in the streets. Thus, a result of multiple marginalization has been the emergence of street gangs and the generation of gang members. The same kinds of pressures and forces that push male youth into gangs also apply to females.

Cultural Alienation Among Asian American Youth

Many of these [Vietnamese] children bear tattoos on their wrists or arms that say *"Han Doi,"* or simply the initials "H.D.", or the word *"Han."* Each means "Resenting Society." Other tattoos that reflect their isolation and pain are *"Doi la So Khong"* (Life Is a Zero); "Tuoi Tre *Thieu Tinh Thuong"* (Youth Lacks Love); or *"Buon vi So Phan"* (I Feel Bad about My Destiny). These marks, often in the form of cigarette burns, are distressingly common on the bodies of the juvenile offenders I counsel.

Whatever the reasons, the juvenile members of gangs are not being integrated into American society. . . .

They create a world of their own in the gang. The surrogate family of the gang offers comradeship, understanding, respect, and approval. The world of street gangs is replete with its own rules, vocabularies, dress codes, tattoos, resources, and insignias. . . .

A California high school student observed, "We have been treated like outsiders. We haven't been accepted by the American culture. Gangs allow us to identify with something."

Patrick Du Phuoc Long, *The Dream Shattered: Vietnamese Gangs in America*. Boston: Northeastern University Press, 1996.

Society and the criminal justice system have so far not fashioned adequate responses to curtail gang growth. Families, schools, and law enforcement merit special scrutiny in this regard for two main reasons. First, they are the primary agents of social control in society. Second, they are uniquely adaptive and responsive to the concerns of society. Although each of these institutions has made its separate contribution to the gang problem, it is their joint actions (or inactions) that make the problem worse. It is in the vacuum of their collective failure that street socialization has taken over and rooted the quasi institution of the street gang.

Families

Family life and parenting practices play the initial role in the socialization of a child. It is within the family that individuals form their first significant relationships, and family training first guides and directs them onto a conventional path of participation in society. In short, parents are the primary caretakers who introduce the child to the world. They gradually expand the child's social space (i.e., from the cradle to the bedroom to the home to the neighborhood) to include other, non-kin influences. Disruptions in family life place stress on parenting practices and duties. In poverty-ridden, ethnic minority communities, these disruptions often result in abbreviated or curtailed supervision and direction of household children. Female gang members are often twice affected, since they generally become single parents—"stroller queens," in the words of one flippant observer. Despite the alarming statistics, however, it must be noted that some of these women successfully navigate a life of poverty, mature out of gangs, and become strong and committed mothers.

Schools

Clearly, educational institutions serve as society's primary arena for turning out citizens and trained members of the workforce. In the United States, schools are next in importance to the family in providing structure and meaning to children's lives and acting as an agency for social control. As a child grows up, schools eventually assume the responsibilities of the family for the bulk of each child's daytime activities.

The members of the ethnic groups included here have come mostly from an immigrant background, and so the U.S. system of formal education is new to them. The shift in care and supervision of a child from family to school, into the hands of non-kin, can be particularly troublesome for those who have migrated to Los Angeles from small communities where they enjoyed extensive kinship networks (which serve to provide what has been called social capital). If stressed parents, now without these networks, are already crippled in socializing their children, then sending them to school under the charge of schoolteachers compounds the problem.

Low-income and ethnic minorities have historically suffered negative, damaging experiences in the educational system. Research shows that standard school policies such as tracking by ability group and the use of standardized tests as the ultimate measure of educational performance and ability have worked against minority students. These students often attend segregated, underfunded, inferior schools, where they encounter cultural insensitivity and an ethnocentric curriculum.

The motivation and strategies for seeking a higher status begin in the family but are formally forged in the educational system and process. In complex societies, schools serve as the mechanism for youths to translate their aspirations into conventional, constructive goals. In terms of reaching for a higher status, many low-income children exhibit a gap between aspirations and expectations. Even though they might have high hopes, they are led (often unaware) to see their goals as outside of their world, exceeding their grasp. Being pragmatic, they assume they won't realize their dreams.

Law Enforcement

The acceptance of the "rightness" of the central social value system is pivotal to social control and citizenship, for individuals are obviously more likely to break the rules if they do not believe in the rules and regulations. Social order depends on the personal internalization of the values of society (the "ought-tos") and of patterned behavior that adheres to the norms of society (the blueprints for action). The latter are first and primarily inculcated by parents, followed by schools, and reinforced early on by peers, especially during the passage from childhood to adulthood.

Youths who are weakly (or not at all) tethered to home and school have weakened ties to society's conventional institutions and values. Because of this deficit, members of law enforcement—the street social-control specialists—often step in as the controlling authority of last resort for our youth. Law enforcement and the criminal justice apparatus serve as the sanctioning source for individuals who consistently fail to conform. When they enter the picture, it is clear that society has not only failed to properly integrate its low-income members but additionally, as we will shortly note, is making it easier for them to become street-socialized.

Street Socialization

Multiple forces working jointly lead to children spending more time on the streets, under the purview and guidance of a multiple-aged peer group. In various Los Angeles ethnic communities, this group often takes the form of the street gang. For girls as well as boys, the street becomes a haven and gang life is romanticized, even though it often ultimately brings them trouble and, for girls, additional victimization. What established gangs in the neighborhood have to offer is nurture, protection, friendship, emotional support, and other ministrations for unattended, unchaperoned resident youth. In other words, street socialization fills the voids left by inadequate parenting and schooling, especially inadequate familial care and supervision. This street-based process molds the youth to conform to the ways of the street. On the streets, the person acquires the models and means for new norms, values, and attitudes.

Macrostructural forces have all too often warped or blocked the educational trajectories of minority children, especially the most marginalized gang youth segments of the population. Dropout rates for ethnic minorities, especially for Latinos and African Americans, are notoriously high, and the children most affected are the street-based ones: in some South Central Los Angeles high schools, the rates are as high as 79 percent. Once out of school, the students drop into gangs and commit to the gang's values and norms.

Street socialization alienates youths from what is learned in the schools, while societal discrimination and economic injustice further erode allegiance to conventional commitments. Boys and girls from these backgrounds are regularly truant from school and organize "ditching parties," a practice that reinforces "we-ness" among street peers. (Ditching parties are get-togethers, often to share drinks or drugs, by adolescents who are "ditching," i.e., illicitly not attending school.). With such a weak educational foundation, coupled with family voids, it is no wonder that a conventional path to a higher status escapes the purview of most gang members. Generally poor job prospects exacerbate the situation for minority youth who already have family and school difficulties.

Through the marginalization and street socialization of urban youth and the creation of a street gang subculture, with values and norms of its own, the street gang becomes a subsociety. Once this subsociety has been created to meet the needs of its creators, it persists and becomes an urban fixture in certain neighborhoods, compelling future generations of youth to join it or otherwise come to terms with it. In these ways, at home and in schools, urban youth acquire a gang-oriented set of rules and regulations.

Gang norms perpetuate a state of male dominance, and females, with few exceptions, largely follow these rules and regulations. Once a member of a gang, a girl or young woman gains status recognition mostly from other homegirls and only occasionally from homeboys. Generally speaking, female street gangs are auxiliaries to the male set. The few autonomous or mixed gangs that exist do not last as long as the auxiliaries, even though the female members continue their street life and associations in another context. Of the few examples cited in the literature, one black female gang in San Francisco was reported to have separated from the males when they discovered that as drug traffickers they could keep all the profits for themselves.

To complicate matters, most of the experiences gang youth have with law enforcement are hostile and antagonistic. For example, special gang units sometimes fan the flames of conflict between rival gangs, police seek and arrest undocumented youths and turn them over to immigration authorities for deportation, and prison guards single out incarcerated gang members for special treatment. Overall, ethnic minority youths, gang or non-gang, resent the "dissing" (disrespect) meted out by patrol officers. These experiences further undermine the recognition and acceptance of the dominant value system, for once youths have begun to reject the law and its underlying values, they often develop a resistance orientation and take a defiant and destructive stance. . . .

Structural Causes

Adaptation and integration into the city for many racially distinct and culturally different newcomers usually entails starting off on the bottom rung of the ladder. However, some groups have had the rungs above them sawed off, in effect. Most of them are therefore unable to move up as quickly or smoothly as, say, white ethnics of the nineteenth-century. Some particularly talented or assertive individuals manage to stretch past gaps in the rungs to make their way up the metaphorical ladder, but others cannot escape the conditions they find themselves in. The persistent pattern of inferior living situations and substandard working conditions that they confront result in major family stresses and strains, deep-rooted schooling barriers and difficulties, and hostile and negative relations and interactions with law enforcement personnel. From this context the street culture and subsociety has emerged.

Structural causes must therefore be at the forefront of any serious discussions on what causes gangs and creates gang members. . . .

Ideally, the solution to the gang problem is linked to resolving all problems arising directly or indirectly from the tremendous social and economic inequalities in our society. Clearly, causes built into the social system are crucial to understanding gangs and gang members, even though not all poverty-stricken children join gangs. But poverty areas generate most gang members, and the poorest of the poor are often more marginalized and thus more subject to street socialization and joining gangs, an indication that even within poverty populations there is internal variation.

As the economic and social system prevalent in the United States increasingly becomes dominant around the globe, gangs likewise are becoming a worldwide phenomena, typically linked to the migration of large numbers of people to cities. The adaptation to cities by already poor people, sometimes made poorer in the transition, too often results in marginalization processes. Studies worldwide indicate that the migration of former peasants and rural workers often carries with it a series of living and working disruptions that strongly undermine traditional social control institutions. . . . Thus, many children in these situations are forced to grow up on the streets. To eliminate this marginalization process and the resultant street socialization would require massive changes in our way of life at the macrostructural level.

> *"Pran's self-esteem was high. He had money
> in his pocket. He had nice clothes to wear,
> and there were lots of girls."*

Young People Join Gangs to Make Money Selling Drugs

Mark D. Freado

Mark D. Freado is the executive director of the American Re-Education Association, a group that helps child development professionals work with troubled youth and their families. In the following viewpoint he tells the story of Pran, a Cambodian-American teen who joined a gang for the chance to emulate his role model—a successful drug dealer and gang leader who always had new cars, clothes, and girls. Pran is typical of many gang members who join for the entrepreneurial opportunities, Freado argues, only to find that such gang involvement is difficult to escape and has serious costs.

As you read, consider the following questions:

1. What did Pran find so attractive about the gangster role model he describes, according to Freado?
2. What benefits did Pran derive from his criminal gang activities, according to the author?
3. Why is leaving a gang so difficult, according to Freado?

Mark D. Freado, "Now It's Time to Pass It On . . ." *Reclaiming Children and Youth*, vol. 11, Fall 2002, pp. 145–46. Edited by Nicholas J. Long and Larry K. Brendtro. Reproduced by permission. For subscription information and to order back issues, contact: Compassion Publishing, Ltd, 3315 N. 124th St., Suite J, Brookfield, WI 53005; phone: 262-317-3430 or 1-800-285-7910; fax: 262-783-2360; email: contact@compassionpublishing.com

This is the story of a youth for whom the drug culture offered an entrepreneurial opportunity, rather than an addictive high. Once enmeshed in the drug business, a young person can face great difficulties making the transition to prosocial roles.

"*He was somebody I looked up to.*" Ten-year-old Pran sat on the step of his apartment building; his eyes were fixed on the man in the shiny new car, dressed in fine clothes. He was well-built, always had a lot of friends around him, and lots of girls. Pran said, "He seemed to have it all together. He was somebody I looked up to."

Pran was finding his role model in a neighborhood gangster and drug dealer. For several years before that, he and his friends would play in a nearby park where it was "just loaded with gangsters." They let the little kids play and didn't bother them. As the kids grew older, they were invited to join. Within two years, Pran belonged to the gang in his northeastern community and began an eight-year odyssey, including drugs, violence, and incarceration.

The Plight of a First Generation American

Having lived in the United States since he was four years old, Pran, a Cambodian-American youngster, was growing up as an American youth struggling with the same inner city pressures of thousands of others. His parents, however, continued to live as Cambodians transplanted to America, not pursuing citizenship primarily because of the language barrier. They never learned English, and Pran knew only enough Khmer to get by at home. His parents were relieved knowing their children would grow up far away from the horrors they knew before they fled Cambodia in the late 1970s.

Pran's relationship with his parents was strained. His father was strict, but absent much of the time because of his work in the second shift evening hours. Pran's mother was less effective with him as he got older and, in addition, she had his two younger siblings for which to care. She was not able to control him as he approached adolescence, and he was drawn to the adventure of the street, developing relationships within his gang.

Relationships in the gang provided Pran with the acknowledgement, affirmation, and sense of the belonging he needed. These relationships sustained him for seven years. Pran developed a particularly strong relationship with Tim, the leader of the gang. Older and more experienced than the others, Tim used his experience, not only to control the gang, but also to teach the ways of the street. Pran was a ready, willing, and capable student.

Drugs were a daily part of the experience of this group of young people. Pran initially resisted marijuana use because of what he learned in school about the harmful effects of drugs. As time passed, he determined that his friends, who smoked pot daily, still seemed to be able to function in a "normal" way. Most of them were able to handle the regular business of the gang, which included violent confrontations with rivals and survival. He eventually gave in to the presence and pressure of the drug and began using regularly as well.

Opportunity for Advancement

After a few months, Tim presented an economic development plan to the gang. They would sell heroin to earn some money to spend, but also to support the gang and buy guns. Tim taught them how to do it right. The locations, the prices, and the process were addressed. They had the best stuff in the city and no lack of customers. Soon he was bringing in as much as $900 each day from his efforts. He set up shop in a park loaded with gangsters, selling to prostitutes and junkies, who would scrape together everything they had. He also sold to "normal looking people," who didn't appear strung out. They tended to buy the most and commented the most on the quality of the product.

Holding the line on the price meant not giving someone a break that was short of the set price. This was always the case unless it involved a really good customer. That was part of what he was taught. He was also taught to offer premiums, an extra bag, for those who brought in five more customers. At the time, he didn't consider the impact on the lives of the people who were his customers. It was just something he didn't think about.

Pran was most focused on what he got out of the enterprise. There were several very significant benefits for him. Spending much of the day at work, Pran received about $20 per day from the proceeds of his sales and that was all right. He was 14 years old, and $20 a day took care of basic things. In addition, because he was so good at what he did, Tim would always give him extra money for things when he asked.

It Wasn't All About the Money

The greater benefits were intangible. He had satisfaction from doing what he was doing very well. He was contributing a great deal to the well-being of the gang. Most importantly, it put him in very good favor with Tim. All of that would eventually help him move up, increasing his status and influence.

Gangs and Drug Trafficking

In the 1990s many violent gangs in New York, Chicago, Miami, Dallas, Cincinnati, and Washington, D.C., have entered the illegal drug business. They are actively spreading drugs and violence to other cities all across the country. In Chicago, where gang membership is now in the thousands, after a lull in the 1970s, the infamous El Rukins gang is under active investigation for drug trafficking. In New York, police are struggling to contain the explosion of drug-related violence. A Miami-based gang called the Untouchables is pushing crack northward to Atlanta, Savannah, and other cities of the Southeast, where the group is known and feared as the Miami Boys. An investigative reports TV documentary on the drug trade shows in detail how gangs have brought drugs from Colombia into a small city like Tyler, Texas.

The gangs' entry into drug trafficking on a major scale may be creating the nation's biggest crime problem in decades. Drug profits are soaring and so is the drug-related homicide rate in cities where the gangs are most entrenched. It is arguable, in fact, that the emergence of drug gangs from coast to coast is very similar to what occurred during the early years of Prohibition, when La Cosa Nostra consolidated its status as an underworld cartel by building on the profits of illicit alcohol.

Lewis Yablonsky, *Gangsters: Fifty Years of Madness, Drugs, and Death on the Streets of America*. New York: New York University Press, 1997.

Pran did not use heroin; it was too dangerous. His financial benefit was minor, considering the volume of drugs and money involved. The value of all this for him was his status in the group and the relationship with its leader. Pran's self-esteem was high. He had money in his pocket. He had nice clothes to wear, and there were lots of girls. He was living in the manner of the role model he identified four years before. He was living the life of the successful gangster and drug dealer.

During this period, Pran ran away from home and began to live with Tim, who provided a room in his family's home for members of his gang to "hang out." Pran would stay there for days at a time. He would periodically go home to check on his mother. After determining that she was all right and listening for a while as she expressed her anger and fear at what he was doing with his life, he went back to the community of the gang.

After months of leading the heroin enterprise, Tim decided that it was too "hot" to continue, and it ended abruptly. A few months later, they began selling marijuana. That, however, did not last because of the popularity of the drug among the gang members, who consumed profits with their own use. Having learned the art and science of selling drugs, Pran began to independently sell marijuana.

Pran was older now and provided some leadership. Instead of staying at Tim's, Pran now stayed in a house rented by one of the other members, and he used the proceeds from his marijuana sales for his own needs and "to help out some of the younger guys." As he generously shared the skills he had learned from a more experienced member of the gang, he was also becoming to others what Tim had been for him.

The Beginning of the End

Pran's gang involvement lasted about eight years, ending in prison. I met him a year before his incarceration, while he was attending an alternative school where I was providing consultation and training. The administrators of the school asked me to see him because he was struggling. He had been attending the school nearly two years and performed very well, achieving academic success and providing positive peer leadership. Just prior to our meeting, he began to be absent more and fell behind in his coursework.

In our initial discussion, Pran talked just a little about his gang involvement and the difficulty he would have disassociating himself from the gang. He told me he enrolled in that school on his own because he wanted to do better for himself. He was very pleased and proud of what he had been able to accomplish. Pran was most appreciative of the support he received from the staff of the school who were willing to give him a chance and believe in him. He allowed them to stay in the room for our discussion, saying, "It's okay, I trust them."

Pran said he was determined to make his life different. He always believed that he could be something other than a gangster, in part because he had values and dreams he acquired from his family and early school experience. He never let go of them, although they were not evident in much of what he had done for many years. There were also the relationships he had with the teachers and administrators at the school. They constantly challenged, encouraged, and supported him.

It's a Rocky Road Out

Pran is still paying for the years he was involved in relationships characterized by violence and drugs. He was unable to complete the alternative school program because he was incarcerated for four years. There is still work to be done to overcome his past. Even in prison, he demonstrated an impressive resilience and determination, and he has now completed his G.E.D.

Pran learned to find strength in relationships that supported his values and dreams. He is still struggling to overcome his past. For nearly a year, he has been working with at-risk youth in his community. Now it is his turn to pass it on, this time in a positive way.

*"Gangs migrate into the minds and lives of
young people through the mass media."*

The Mass Media Influence
Young People to Join Gangs

Mike Carlie

Mike Carlie is a professor of sociology and criminal justice
at Southwest Missouri State University at Springfield. The
following viewpoint is excerpted from his book *Into the Abyss:
A Personal Journey into the World of Street Gangs.* The book
was based on two years of research during which Carlie rode
with police gang units and talked with gang members as well
as their parents, teachers, and probation and parole officers.
In the viewpoint Carlie argues that the media often paint a
glamorous picture of the gang lifestyle and teach impres-
sionable youths how to behave like gang members—including how to shoot up drugs and settle disputes with violence.

As you read, consider the following questions:

1. What does Carlie fear American youth might learn from
   watching the movie *American History X*?
2. What side does the author take in the debate over
   whether watching media violence causes people to
   become violent?
3. How does Carlie apply findings about the relationship
   between violence in the media and violence among
   America's youth to media portrayals of gangs and youths'
   attraction to gangs?

Mike Carlie, *Into the Abyss: A Personal Journey into the World of Street Gangs.*
Springfield, MO: Self Publication, 2002. Copyright © 2002 by Michael K. Carlie.
All rights reserved. Reproduced by permission.

Gangs migrate into the minds and lives of young people through the mass media. The term "Mass media" refers here to the Internet, radio, television, commercial motion pictures, videos, CDs, and the press (newspapers, journals, and magazines)—what are referred to collectively as broadcast and print media. Their impact on the minds of our youth has been hotly debated. I believe media portrayals which glorify gang behavior do little to help reduce our youth's interest in gangs. . . .

Movies and videos which show gang members enjoying the fruits of their illegal activities (i.e., drugs, sex, a nice apartment or house, money, cars, power, guns) suggest, in some children's minds, ways to reach the goal to which most Americans aspire—financial success and all it entails. The ways in which that income is earned often entails the use of violence. [Television producer David Fanning writes]:

> Before the age of eighteen, the average American teen will have witnessed eighteen thousand simulated murders on TV. While staggering in number, more disturbing is the effect this steady diet of imaginary violence may have on America's youth.
>
> Over the past forty years, more than three thousand studies have investigated the connection between television violence and real violence . . . Though none conclude a direct cause and effect relationship, it becomes clear that watching television is one of a number of important factors affecting aggressive behavior.

By watching mass media portrayals of gang member behavior, some children learn of illegitimate ways to acquire goods and services. They learn how to lay in wait to "hit" (execute) someone. They learn what a drive-by-shooting looks like—how it's done and how to possibly get away without getting caught. If they watched *American History X*, they learned how to "curb" someone.

If you didn't see *American History X*, here's what it shows—in full color and in all its gory detail. A Skinhead (a Caucasian gang known for its ideologically-based hatred of African-Americans and other minorities) is shown forcing an African-American youth to lay face-down in the street perpendicular to the curb. The youth's mouth is then forced open and pushed down until the curb is in his mouth. The skinhead then stomped on the back of the young man's neck, fracturing his jaw, shattering his teeth, and breaking his neck. . . .

A Hot Debate

The impact of the media on the minds of our youth is hotly debated. The debate goes like this . . .

There are those who believe only children who are predisposed to violence will be stimulated by it when shown in the media. Some believe otherwise non-violent children learn to be violent by watching violence, particularly when it is observed without the supervision of someone who explains that certain kinds of violence are inappropriate and wrong. Finally, there are those who believe violence in the media releases one's feelings of anger and violence by providing catharsis (in this case, a purging of one's own anger).

Gangsta Rap Glamorizes Gangs

The debasement of our culture, of which gangsta rap is a big part, has coarsened children in general and put high-risk kids in a dangerous place. Taking drugs, carrying guns and disrespecting human beings is now not only socially acceptable in many situations, it is downright glamorous.

Bill O'Reilly, *New York Daily News*, March 7, 2004.

Which is right? I think they all are. I believe there are children who are raised in violence and who, when they observe violence or other gang activity in the media, view the media portrayal as confirmation of what they already know. If you have a problem just put your fist in it and it will go away.

I also believe there are unsupervised children who, fed a constant diet of television and rap music violence, begin to emulate it, particularly if there are others who are doing the same thing. Every child wants to be accepted. If I am rejected by the "good kids," perhaps the "bad kids" will want me if I act and think like they do. And there are those who feel frustration and anger who, after a media portrayal of violence, feel purged of such feelings.

When I read about the relationship between violence in the media and violence among our youth I extrapolate the findings and think of them in regard to gangs. When it comes to the portrayal of gangs and gang members, the mass media sometimes go into great detail. They portray the language, dress, body movements, and look of a gang member— male and female. They show, in explicit detail, the crimes gang members commit—how drugs are sold, how to "shoot up" (inject drugs intravenously), how to free base, how to rape someone, how to stab or shoot someone, how to settle disputes using violence. The list is very long. The problem is that it is the wrong list in terms of socializing our youth into acceptable, legal behaviors.

The impact of media portrayals of gangs and the activities of their members help us understand why gangs form.

> "*Young people join gangs for a variety of reasons, which can be influenced by conditions in their family, school and neighborhood.*"

Young People Are Drawn to Gangs for Multiple Reasons

California Attorney General's Office, Crime and Violence Prevention Center

In 1952 the California Attorney General's office established the Crime Prevention Center to stimulate resource development in crime prevention policy. The organization was renamed the Crime and Violence Prevention Center (CVPC) in 1994 to emphasize its commitment to helping communities develop long-term solutions to the problems of crime and violence. The following selection is taken from a 2003 publication by the CVPC on gangs. The authors of the report point to many different reasons young people join gangs, ranging from poverty to escaping a difficult family situation to protecting themselves from being victims of gang crimes.

As you read, consider the following questions:

1. What is the educational background of gang members, according to the authors?
2. What similarities do the authors see between 1940s society and today in terms of causes of gang behavior?
3. Why do young people join or start gangs, according to the authors?

California Attorney General's Office, Crime and Violence Prevention Center, *Gangs: A Community Response*, June 2003.

No one is immune from the impact that gangs can have on a community. Gang violence is widespread, dangerous and deadly in many California communities.

Gangs are not a big-city or an inner-city problem, any more than they are a problem of a particular race or culture. Gangs cross all racial, ethnic, socio-economic and geographic boundaries. Gangs are not gender specific. They exist in urban, suburban and rural communities.

While many who join gangs are unmarried, unemployed and school dropouts, today's gang members can also be parents, students, employed and educated. In fact, some gang members are honor students in high school, college students and even active members of the U.S. military.

Belonging to a gang severely harms a young person's future. Gang members often socialize only with other gang members, reinforcing their limited view of life. They frequently establish a lifelong pattern of involvement with the criminal justice system. They may commit serious and violent crimes that lead to lengthy incarcerations. They may be injured for life, or killed. Their gang membership may place an entire family household at risk. Gang members who do make it to adulthood sometimes become dependent on alcohol and drugs. For some, the gang lifestyle is passed down as a family tradition leading to generational gangs.

To prevent the devastation of crime and violence caused by gangs, and of lost human potential by so many young people, we must respond together, as parents, family members, friends and community. The first step is to take a candid look at our own families and the community around us. Understanding and accepting what might be happening even within our own families is an important step that helps us prepare an effective personal and community response. . . .

California Gang History

Although the nation's first modern-day criminal street gangs—of Irish, Italian and Jewish descent—formed in the early 1800's in the Five Points area of New York, the first California gangs formed in the early 1900's in the Los Angeles area.

Even though California-based gangs are not the oldest in

the nation, they are probably the most copied of all gangs. In California, early Mexican gangs became the model for all other gangs that followed.

Early California gang members were caught between two worlds. Their Mexican heritage provided a rich, family-oriented culture, but Western customs and education forced a change in these young people that caused stress within the traditional family structure. While attempting to adapt to this change, the children became strangers both to their own families and to their new homeland because they were not fully accepted into the culture.

Ramirez. © 2002 by Copley News Service. Reproduced by permission.

Add social dysfunctions, such as class distinction, bias and prejudice, and an "us versus them" attitude developed. The result is that some of these young people formed gangs. Initially, most gangs formed for protection, but quickly as gang membership grew, rivalries developed and violence escalated. While violence in the early 1940's involved fist fighting, today it includes extremely violent and deadly acts, often perpetrated with guns.

Even in today's 21st Century society, immigrant or refugee groups can experience alienation. While social and cultural family stress has been a factor in the formation of many different types of gangs, it is not the sole reason that gangs form. Joining and maintaining membership in a gang is motivated by many other reasons. . . .

Why Youth Join Gangs

Young people join gangs for a variety of reasons, which can be influenced by conditions in their family, school and neighborhood. A vulnerable child seeks love, protection and the acceptance of his or her peers. Youth, who lack parental guidance and support, or opportunities for positive involvement with their peers, often turn to a gang to meet these needs. Once a child is lost to a gang, it is hard to get him or her back because the gang can literally become a surrogate family for that young person. The loyalties, love and dedication normally found in traditional nuclear families are transferred to the gang family. Members can develop intense bonds with other members and feel a need to protect them. Many times, problems at home act as a cohesive factor for gang members.

Other reasons for joining a gang include: excitement, physical protection, peer pressure, family tradition, perceived financial gain, an avenue to gain "respect," being wanted and valued by a group, being feared by others, getting girl friends, gaining notoriety or out of boredom. Many gang members doubt their ability to achieve at school or to obtain job skills and employment. Many prospective gang members are youth who are not successful at school and are not receiving the attention and support they feel they need from their family.

Gang involvement and violence may be symptomatic of family, social or psychological dysfunction. The impact of these problems can be prevented and minimized by authority figures and community leaders understanding the dynamics of gang behavior. This understanding includes learning how to deal with gang behaviors and finding out what alternatives and resources are available to change them.

Periodical Bibliography

The following articles have been selected to supplement the diverse views presented in this chapter.

Leon Bing	"Homegirls," *Rolling Stone*, April 12, 2001.
G. David Curry	"Female Gang Involvement, *Journal of Research in Crime and Delinquency*, February 1998.
Tiffany Danitz	"Keeping Kids Out of Gangs," *Insight on the News*, July 6–13, 1998.
Richard L. Dukes, Ruben O. Martinez, and Judith A. Stein	"Precursors and Consequences of Membership in Youth Gangs," *Youth and Society*, December 1997.
Tom Hayden	"Gato and Alex—No Safe Place," *Nation*, July 10, 2000.
Xiaoming Li et al.	"Risk and Protective Factors Associated with Gang Involvement Among Urban African-American Adolescents," *Youth & Society*, December 2002.
Kelly McEvers and Linnet Myers	"Women of 'The World,'" *Chicago Tribune*, March 26, 1999.
Mary E. Pattillo	"Sweet Mothers and Gangbangers," *Social Forces*, March 1998.
Colin Powell	"I Wasn't Left to Myself," *Newsweek*, April 27, 1998.
Isis Sapp-Grant and Rosemarie Robotham	"Gang Girl: The Transformation of Isis Sapp-Grant," *Essence*, August 1998.
Douglas E. Thompkins	"School Violence: Gangs and a Culture of Fear," *The Annals of the American Academy of Political and Social Science*, January 2000.
Kevin M. Thompson and Rhonda Braaten Antrim	"Youth Maltreatment and Gang Involvement," *Journal of Interpersonal Violence*, June 1998.
Chanequa J. Walker-Barnes and Craig A. Mason	"Perceptions of Risk Factors for Female Gang Involvement Among African American and Hispanic Women," *Youth & Society*, March 2001.

CHAPTER 3

How Can the Legal System Best Reduce Gang Violence?

Chapter Preface

On January 7, 1999, Karen Clarke and her eight-year-old son, Leroy "BJ" Brown, were ambushed and killed in front of their Bridgeport, Connecticut, home. BJ was to testify against gang leader Russell Peeler, who was being charged with the May 1998 murder of Rudy Snead, the boyfriend of BJ's mother. In December 1998 the trial court ordered the release of the prosecution's witness list to Peeler's attorney. Less than a month later, BJ and his mother were killed. Peeler is serving a life sentence for their murder without possibility of parole.

Witness intimidation, which can, as evidenced by the Peeler case, lead to murder, creates tremendous obstacles for those who prosecute gang members. According to Robert McCulloch, president of the National District Attorneys Association, "Prosecutors across the country believe that the issue of witness intimidation is the single biggest hurdle facing any successful gang prosecution." To ensure that the testimony of witnesses to gang crimes is properly admitted into evidence, prosecutors must preserve the defendant's rights to a fair, public trial. However, balancing the defendant's rights with the right of a witness to testify without fear of retaliation is often difficult because the legal system gives greater priority to the rights of the accused than to the rights of witnesses.

Some jurisdictions have developed tools that protect the rights of defendants and still encourage witnesses to testify. For example, in New York, in extraordinary circumstances such as cases involving violent gang-related crime, prosecutors are allowed to withhold the names of witnesses until they take the stand. Maryland's gang prosecutors argue that witness addresses need not be disclosed as long as the witness can be made available to the defense. In one case, Maryland prosecutors provided a witness's name but obtained a protection order barring the defense attorney from revealing the identity of the witness to the defendant, his brother, or their acquaintances. The witness had evidence connecting the defendant to a double murder that had been witnessed by more than three hundred other people, none of whom were willing to testify because they feared retaliation.

Courtroom witness intimidation is another problem gang prosecutors face. Judge William B. Spellbring Jr. explains: "In the courtroom sometimes, you see a whole group of street kids, and you know they're connected to one side, probably the defendant's. . . . They just sit in the back of the courtroom—you can see them give the witness the evil eye." Judges such as Spellbring cannot simply close the courtroom to gang members. Both the Sixth and the Fourteenth Amendment to the U.S. Constitution guarantee the defendant's right to a public trial. In some jurisdictions, however, if prosecutors can provide evidence that an open court would endanger a witness or compromise testimony, they may close the court to the public or exclude individual gang members. The North Carolina State Code, for example, allows judges to "impose reasonable limitations on access to the courtroom when necessary to ensure the orderliness of the courtroom proceedings or the safety of the persons present."

The rules of evidence can also create obstacles for gang prosecutors. One such rule prevents the admission of written statements made by witnesses who cannot corroborate these statements on the witness stand. In gang prosecutions, these witnesses are sometimes murdered to prevent their testifying, thus some claim that the evidentiary rule encourages defendants to kill potential witnesses. In 1994 eight or more potential witnesses against a Washington, D.C., gang known as the First Street Crew were murdered. As a result of this case, evidentiary rules were changed. Even though the defense has no opportunity to cross-examine murdered witnesses, a constitutionally protected right, D.C. prosecutors can now enter into evidence the statements of slain witnesses if they can show that these witnesses were killed to keep them from testifying. The D.C. Court of Appeals held, "The defendant who has removed an adverse witness is in a weak position to complain about losing the chance to cross-examine him."

Whether or not these strategies will encourage witnesses to testify against gang members is subject to dispute. In the following chapter authors debate the impact other legal system strategies have on gangs and the communities they inhabit.

"*It is time for Congress to focus on this problem [of gangs] and address it at the national level.*"

A National Law Enforcement Strategy Is Needed to Combat Gangs

Dianne Feinstein

Dianne Feinstein is a Democratic senator from California, a state known for its problems with gangs. In October 2003 she, along with Republican Senator Orrin Hatch of Utah, introduced a bill that would increase funding for federal law enforcement and provide for more federal prosecutions of gang members, including juveniles. In the following viewpoint she argues that such a federal strategy against gangs is necessary because gangs have spread beyond cities in California and other states to become a nationwide problem.

As you read, consider the following questions:

1. What examples of innocent victims of gang violence does Feinstein describe?
2. How much has gang membership risen nationally, according to the author?
3. What are some of the provisions of the Gang Prevention and Effective Deterrence Act that Feinstein has introduced?

Dianne Feinstein, "Congress Must Address Upsurge in Gangs," *Los Angeles Daily News*, March 10, 2004. Copyright © 2004 by *Los Angeles Daily News*, Los Angeles Newspaper Group. Reproduced by permission.

On Sept. 10, 2003, two students at Manual Arts High School in South Los Angeles, Demario Moore and Quinesha Dunford, were standing on a sidewalk with a group of friends when a car full of gang members drove by and started firing bullets at the crowd.

Within hours, the two teenagers—neither of whom was involved with gangs—were dead.

Innocent young people like Demario and Quinesha are killed nearly every day in the United States by gangs who terrorize their communities. These senseless attacks are usually targeted at competing gang members, but gangs are increasingly becoming more brazen.

Just last month [February 2004], Los Angeles police Officer Ricardo Lizarraga was shot while responding to a domestic-violence call in the Leimert Park neighborhood. A short time later, he died at a nearby hospital, the victim of a reputed gang member's bullet.

In recent years, gangs have become more sophisticated and more violent criminal enterprises. What were once loosely organized groups centered around dealing illegal drugs within a particular neighborhood are now complex criminal organizations whose activities include weapons trafficking, gambling, smuggling, robbery and, of course, homicide.

In 2002, over half of the 1,228 homicides committed in Los Angeles County were gang-related. Similarly, over half of the 499 murders committed in the city of Los Angeles during 2003 were the result of gang violence.

Conservative estimates put the number of separate street gangs in L.A. County at approximately 1,000 and the number of gang members at around 150,000. To the south, Orange County has an estimated 20,000 gang members and comparable numbers of gang members exist in Ventura and San Bernardino counties

Gangs Spread Beyond California

The reach of gangs, however, extends far beyond Southern California.

Indeed, Los Angeles serves as a "source city" whose gang members migrate to other communities across the country and set up new criminal entities.

One such operation, the L.A.-based 18th Street Gang, is known to have initiated gang activities all over California, in Southwest border and Pacific Northwest states, and in East Coast states including New Jersey and New York.

War on Terrorists Should Include Gangs

There has been much talk since 9/11 of sleeper cells, Islamic terrorists waiting among us for the word to be given so that they can go out and murder as many Americans as possible.

But there are other terrorists among us who are not at all hard to find and who, like the Ku Klux Klan once did, rule with violence. In Los Angeles, there are well-known street gangs that have murdered 10,000 people over the past 20 years! . . .

It seems to me that if President [George W.] Bush wants to wage total war on terrorists, he should include these home-grown knuckleheads with the others and move, in conjunction with local law enforcement and community leaders, to eliminate their violent grip on the lives of Americans. Such a vision of law and order would be truly revolutionary.

Stanley Crouch, Knight-Ridder/Tribune Service, July 15, 2003.

In Virginia, a 22-year-old California man was recently charged with recruiting minors into a gang after being arrested at a high school for possession of a loaded gun. The man, a convicted sex offender, had been talking to a 15-year-old student in the school's parking lot when a school security officer called police.

Gang members successfully lure young recruits with offers of protection and easy money. But the gang recruiters have another goal in mind—more young gang members who, if arrested, will face lighter sentences for drug trafficking, assault and other serious crimes.

The result of these aggressive recruitment efforts is a dramatic increase in gang membership nationally, rising from a 1980 estimate of 100,000 to more than 750,000 today. And even as Americans have enjoyed decreases in overall crime for a decade now, gangs have taken a stronger grip on our cities and even many rural communities. Gangs have never been more common, more dangerous or more mobile than they are today.

A National Law Enforcement Solution

To address the gang problem nationwide, Sen. Orrin Hatch, R-Utah, and I have introduced the Gang Prevention and Effective Deterrence Act.[1] The bill:

- Authorizes $650 million over the next five years—$450 million to support federal, state and local law enforcement efforts against violent gangs, and $200 million for intervention and prevention programs for at-risk youths.
- Increases funding for federal prosecutors and FBI agents to strengthen coordinated enforcement efforts against violent gangs.
- Creates new criminal gang prosecution offenses to prohibit recruitment of minors in a criminal street gang, and to punish violent crimes related to gangs.
- Enhances existing gang and violent crime penalties to deter and punish illegal street gangs, and proposes violent crime reforms needed to prosecute gang members effectively.
- Enacts a limited reform of the juvenile justice system to facilitate federal prosecution of 16- and 17-year-old gang members who commit serious acts of violence.

Recently, Los Angeles Police Chief William Bratton likened gang violence to a sleeping tiger. At a two-day gang-violence summit held in January [2004], Bratton warned, "When this tiger awakens it's going to explode, and many communities aren't prepared for it. And we have a national government, a Congress, that is not focused on the problem."

As we've seen from the recent shootings of Demario Moore, Quinesha Dunford and Officer Lizarraga, this sleeping tiger is already lashing out at innocent victims. Gangs present a lethal threat to communities across California and across the nation. And Chief Bratton is right—it is time for Congress to focus on this problem and address it at the national level.

---

1. As of September 2004, the bill had not become law.

> *"After millions of dollars sunk into gang prevention . . . and prosecution, not only have we not managed to solve the gang problem, but it's grown worse."*

A National Law Enforcement Strategy Is an Inadequate Solution to the Problem of Gangs

Mariel Garza

Mariel Garza is a columnist and writer for the *Los Angeles Daily News*. In the following viewpoint she argues that the problem of gangs in Los Angeles has grown worse despite the millions of dollars spent on antigang actions by law enforcement. She questions whether simply spending greater resources on federal and local law enforcement will be effective in reducing gang violence. Unless society re-evaluates its war on gangs and addresses social causes such as inner-city poverty, the problem of gangs will get worse, she predicts.

As you read, consider the following questions:
1. How has the problem of gangs changed since the release of the 1988 movie *Colors*, according to Garza?
2. What doubts does the author express about senator Dianne Feinstein's proposed Gang Prevention and Effective Deterrence Act of 2003?
3. What future scenario does Garza envision?

Mariel Garza, "War on Gangs: Getting Tough Just Isn't Enough," *Los Angeles Daily News*, December 7, 2003, p. V1. Copyright © 2004 by *Los Angeles Daily News*, Los Angeles Newspaper Group. Reproduced by permission.

"We gangs of L.A. will never die . . . just multiply," rapped Ice-T—rather prophetically, it turns out—in the opening scenes of the movie "Colors."

This seminal film about Los Angeles street gangs opened in the spring of 1988 to much controversy, public condemnation and civic soul-searching. After a few scattered incidents of violence that may or may not have been related, some theaters banned the movie, fearful of attracting real gangsters in their blue Crips or red Bloods bandannas. Community groups slammed the depiction of street life, saying it glorified gangsters and their criminal lifestyles.

I saw "Colors" in San Francisco with a college friend, who had grown up in the black neighborhoods of Los Angeles that were the focus of the movie.

A Shocking Film

It was a slice of real life for him, though with some annoyingly goofy Hollywooding-up. Not so for me. Like many non-Angelenos, I was shocked by the graphic violence depicted in the tale of two Los Angeles Police Department [LAPD] officers, members of the the now-disgraced and disbanded anti-gang, CRASH units, which stood for Community Resources Against Street Hoodlums. I was on the edge of my seat.

"Colors" was groundbreaking, defining for the first time to America the truly terrifying levels of gangsterism in Los Angeles—70,000 gang members, 387 gang murders the year before, a police force woefully under-equipped.

How quaint it all seemed when I caught the flick on TV the other night, now an Angeleno used to living with entrenched gang activity—the taggings, shootings and LAPD helicopters waking me up in the middle of the night.

How quaint, and utterly depressing.

Fifteen years after the opening of "Colors," after countless wars declared on the ever-growing numbers of street gang members, after millions of dollars sunk into gang prevention, intervention, detection and prosecution, not only have we not managed to solve the gang problem, but it's grown worse—much worse.

The Bloods and Crips are still here, as are growing numbers of Latino gangs. There are now more than 100,000 identified gang members in Los Angeles. In 2002, Los Angeles was the murder capital of the country, with 658 killings, 334 of them gang-related.

Federal Anti-Gang Laws Do Not Help

Gang legislation is often passed in an overheated emotional atmosphere that is not appropriate to sound policy-making. . . .

While gangs are a serious problem, they are not cause for panic. Youth gangs in the United States first appeared around 1783. Youth gang activity in the United States has had four major peaks: the late 1800s; the 1920s; the 1960s; and the 1990s. It is only in the 1990s that Congress has decided that the gang problem must be addressed through Congress intruding itself on the traditional state function of criminal justice.

Everything gangs do, such as sell controlled substances, kill rival gang members, and steal property, is already illegal under state and federal law. But because the enactment of legislation is often confused with genuine action, enacting "anti-gang" legislation may have a strong political appeal, even when the criminal law has already covered everything that gangs do. When there are no substantive laws that can be added (e.g., since murder and drug dealing are already illegal), legislatures are tempted to create what might be called "second order laws." That is, laws which take existing laws, and arrange them into new combinations, to create new "crimes" from the new combinations. These laws are superfluous and misleading, because they give the public the impression that something is being done, when actually the legislature is doing little more than stamping its feet, and saying that something illegal is illegal again.

David B. Kopel, *Barry Law Review*, 2000.

The firepower used by gang members is even more sophisticated and deadly, and the LAPD remains a very thin blue line. CRASH doesn't exist any more, and the department operates under a federal consent decree after a scandal that exposed the Rampart Division anti-gang unit to be about as criminal as the gangs.

I turned to Los Angeles gang expert Wes McBride to help me understand what's gone wrong. A retired L.A. County Sheriff's Department sergeant, McBride worked gang crimes for years in East Los Angeles, and now shares what he's learned as a president of the California Gang Investigators Association.

No Easy Answers

"There's no easy answer," McBride said. Most of the problem has been a lack of real commitment to prevention programs, he said. We throw money at them for a few months or years, then forget about them. Our enforcement efforts roller-coaster from one extreme to another without any consistency.

But it hasn't stopped people from trying to stop gangs through other means.

At the moment [December 2003], California Sen. Dianne Feinstein is pushing Congress to adopt the Gang Prevention and Effective Deterrence Act of 2003. It would provide $650 million over five years for anti-gang efforts by law enforcement, much of it likely ending up in California to fund well-meaning programs such as those administered by Sheriff Lee Baca, LAPD Chief William Bratton and others.

While I recognize the need for more gang-fighting programs, injunctions, prosecutions, whatever it takes, I've got some serious doubts that any of it will do much more than fill up the jails with gang members—for a time.

Searching for a New Approach

Hasn't it occurred to someone that perhaps we've been going about this all wrong? When you've spent more than two decades in a losing battle, it might make sense to regroup and re-evaluate, perhaps look deeper at the problem.

"We don't address the social causation factors very well," McBride said. "Parents don't give a damn about kids, for one. You can't legislate that, And we're certainly not solving poverty. No matter what people say, gangs stem from poverty."

Unless we start getting a handle on some of these larger issues, the next 15 years aren't likely to see much of an improvement in convincing kids not to join gangs. They're just an outgrowth of the realities of our society. More and more, law-abiding urban citizens will turn to isolationism, to gated communities and private security, or move to safe suburbs.

And the gang-infested neighborhoods will get worse.

It could become like the movie "Escape From New York," McBride jokes, when the law-abiding citizens left town and the urban core was turned into a giant prison with the inmates left to fend for themselves.

It's like a war, you know what I'm saying.
People don't even understand.
They don't even know what they dealing with.
You wanna get rid of the gangs it's gonna take a lot of work,
But people don't understand the size of this,
This is no joke, man, this is real.

Fifteen years, and Ice-T's anthem is more apropos than ever.

"*Federal and state prosecutors are employing [traditional] tools and experimenting with new ones as they fight to wrest communities from the grasp of . . . gangs.*"

Laws Against Gang Activities Reduce Gang Violence

John Gibeaut

Law enforcement officials use state and federal laws to prosecute illegal gang activities and reduce gang violence, claims John Gibeaut in the following viewpoint. Federal prosecutors use the Racketeer Influenced and Corrupt Organizations Act (RICO) to convict gang leaders who conspire to traffic in drugs and murder informants, asserts Gibeaut. States such as California maintain that gang activities such as associating in public violate public nuisance laws. Injunctions against such activities reduce gang violence because when prohibited from associating, gang members have a difficult time conducting illegal activities, Gibeaut contends. Gibeaut is an *ABA Journal* reporter.

As you read, consider the following questions:

1. In Gibeaut's opinion, what organizations was RICO originally designed to prosecute?
2. What are the advantages of federal over state prosecutions, in the author's view?
3. Why did the California Supreme Court reject a First Amendment challenge to a Rocksprings, California, injunction that barred gang members from associating?

John Gibeaut, "Gang Busters," *ABA Journal*, January 1998, pp. 64–68. Copyright © 1998 by the American Bar Association. All rights reserved. Reproduced by permission.

To federal prosecutors, the case against Darryl "Pops" Johnson boiled down to his coldly calculated business decisions.

As a high-ranking member of Chicago's Black Gangster Disciple Nation street gang, Johnson made a business decision when he ordered the May 7, 1995, murder of Darryl "Blunt" Johnson, said Assistant U.S. Attorney Matthew C. Crowl to a jury in early November [1997]. Likewise, Crowl said, Johnson made a business decision when he ordered the murder a month later of Charles "Jello" Banks, who was gunned down on the same South Side street corner where Blunt Johnson was killed.

Pops Johnson suspected that Blunt Johnson, who was not related to the defendant, and Banks had become federal informants against the gang's crack cocaine-dealing operation after they had been arrested on drug charges themselves.

It turned out that Pops Johnson's suspicions were right. Just before Banks was slain, his information enabled authorities to get a court order to tap Pops Johnson's telephone. Prosecutors said Blunt Johnson also had tried to strike a deal with the government but was killed first.

The trial was the fourth in a series of cases arising from the governments investigation of the Gangster Disciples, believed to be the nation's largest and best organized street gang, with as many as 30,000 members. The gang's leader, convicted murderer Larry Hoover, 47, already had been nailed by a federal jury in May [1997] for running the Gangster Disciples' $100 million-a-year drug enterprise from an Illinois prison, where he had been serving two life sentences since 1973.

In Pops Johnson's case, the jury in U.S. District Court took just four hours to convict him of 39 charges, including four counts of ordering the murders, along with conspiring to sell drugs and operating a continuing criminal enterprise. The jury took another two days to tell Judge Suzanne B. Conlon to sentence the 34-year-old Johnson to death by lethal injection.

Expanding the War Against Gangs

Thus ended another battle in the ever-expanding state and federal war against street gangs. As in other legal skirmishes around the nation, the Gangster Disciples prosecution used broad-based statutes, informants and conspiracy evidence to attack one of any gang's most vulnerable spots: the loyalty of its members.

Federal and state prosecutors are employing those tools and experimenting with new ones as they fight to wrest communities from the grasp of increasingly more violent and more populous street gangs. Law enforcement officials are especially busy in the Chicago area and in Southern California, far and away the nation's most active gang regions, according to U.S. Department of Justice figures.

There and elsewhere, today's sophisticated gangs no longer evoke the image of cigarette-smoking, hubcap-stealing hoodlums hanging out on street corners. Gangs aren't kid stuff.

"People assume that gangs mean teen-agers and juveniles," says FBI agent Kenneth E. New, chief of the bureau's Safe Streets/Gangs Unit, which runs 40 multi-agency gang enforcement task forces throughout the nation. "But that's just not true. When you have a Black Gangster Disciple Nation, the leaders are all adults. Hoover's no spring chicken."

As the gangs become more refined, so, too, have law enforcement tools for dealing with them. At the federal level, the Racketeer Influenced and Corrupt Organization Act [RICO] and related conspiracy statutes have become the preferred weapons for removing gang leaders from the streets.

Originally designed for traditional mobsters and white-collar crooks, RICO is ideally suited for street gangs, says the 1970 statute's author, Notre Dame University law Professor G. Robert Blakey.

"They're in the process of growing into Mafias," says Blakey, formerly a lawyer for the Justice Department's Organized Crime and Racketeering Section. "The Mafia started out as a street gang."

In California, which dwarfs the rest of the nation in gang activity, state prosecutors and municipal attorneys have succeeded in using public nuisance laws to obtain injunctions that prevent targeted gang members from congregating in public.

"It is my belief that it should be used everywhere," says Michael Genelin, head of the Los Angeles County District Attorney's Hard-Core Gang Division. "It's the strongest new weapon we have against gangs."

In Illinois, however, the state supreme court recently dealt gang enforcement efforts a setback when it declared unconstitutional a Chicago anti-gang loitering ordinance with similar goals. City attorneys plan to take the case to the U.S. Supreme Court.[1]

Netting the Big Fish

But it may be on the federal front where prosecutors are scoring their most significant victories. Since the early 1990s, the Justice Department has steadily turned up the heat on street gangs with charges brought under RICO and similar statutes.

"In the last two or three years we're seeing more gang cases prosecuted this way, and we are emphasizing that in our training," says Bruce Delaplaine, deputy chief of the Justice Department's Terrorism and Violent Crime Section.

Federal prosecutors have secured indictments and won convictions against street gang leaders from Shreveport, La., to Providence, R.I. In New York City, prosecutors estimate that they have successfully used RICO and similar federal statutes in recent years against some 200 defendants involved in 300 murders. In Chicago, federal charges came down against nearly 200 reputed gang leaders from 1995 to 1997.

With that strategy, the government rarely loses. Prosecutors in Chicago could recall only one recent acquittal in a gang case.

Punishment is swift and severe, usually with mandatory life sentences going to those convicted of the most serious charges. Federal prosecutors also make defendants toe a hard line when it comes to plea bargaining, requiring testimony against other gang members in exchange for leniency.

Unlike state authorities, the federal government has sizable resources to protect and relocate witnesses. Federal prosecution also enables the government to scatter convicted gang leaders in prisons throughout the country, so they don't become concentrated and take control of state prison systems.

1. In 1999 the Supreme Court held in *Chicago v. Morales* that the Chicago anti-gang loitering ordinance was unconstitutional as written.

The Advantages of Federal Prosecution

When a defendant is charged by federal prosecutors with participating in a conspiracy, mountains of evidence come before a jury that usually would be barred as overly prejudicial or irrelevant in a state court trial. That's because the government, besides proving underlying or predicate charges, also must prove that the conspiracy existed and that the defendant participated in it.

Thus, a federal jury likely will hear about a series of murders or other crimes linked to the conspiracy. On the flip side, if Gangster Disciple member Pops Johnson had been charged in state court, he probably would have been tried separately for each murder, and jurors in each case would not have been told about the other.

"I think it certainly makes a more attractive case in the jury's eyes that these are really bad people who need to be prosecuted to the fullest extent of the law," Delaplaine says. "If you were just trying a homicide case, you typically would not be able to get in the evidence that these people are part of an organization."

Use of broad-based charges also enables federal prosecutors to boost the credibility of their chief witnesses, typically informants, also known as "flippers," who testify against gang leaders in exchange for sentence reductions in their own cases. The rationale is simple enough: An informant who may have participated in several murders and drug deals does not look so bad when testifying against the larger organization.

Still, prosecutors say, it is crucial to keep informants honest through other witnesses, such as ordinary citizens and police officers. Wiretaps also play a key role in bolstering informants' credibility because defendants often hang themselves with their own words.

Turning the Tables

Jack Hynes, supervisor of the Cook County State's Attorney's Gang Prosecution Unit in Chicago, recalls how members of the city's El Rukn gang nearly succeeded in sabotaging the federal cases against them with allegations that some cooperating witnesses received drugs and intimate visits with their girlfriends while they were jailed.

The Justice Department fired the lead prosecutor, William Hogan Jr., in 1995 for failing to disclose two witnesses' positive drug tests to defense lawyers. Dozens of the 65 defendants charged in the case won new trials or negotiated lenient sentences the second time around.

Where the Gangs Are

Area	Percent Reporting Gang Activity
Cities with population greater than or equal to 250,000	100 percent
Cities with population between 100,000 and 249,999	85 percent
Cities with population between 50,000 and 99,999	65 percent
Cities with population between 25,000 and 49,999	44 percent
Cities with population between 2,500 and 24,999	20 percent
Suburban counties	35 percent
Rural counties	11 percent

Arlen Egley Jr. and Aline K. Major, *Highlights of the 2001 National Youth Gang Survey*, April 2003.

"I think the lessons that were learned in the El Rukn case can be learned across the country," says Hynes, whose office works with the U.S. attorney in addition to prosecuting gang members in state court. "A flipper is not your friend. You keep them at arm's length. You substantiate what they say, and you document what you give them."

The government evidently had learned that lesson by the time it began prosecuting the Gangster Disciples.

As a result, defense lawyers often are left with little to go on. Sometimes all they can do is argue that the government is overreaching to snare relatively minor players while in search of the big fish. Chicago lawyer Frank Lipuma, for one, says his client, Kevin Williams, is one of the hapless underlings snagged in the Gangster Disciple dragnet, and he now faces a life sentence for his conviction.

"These penalties apply to everyone, from the guy who's

putting all the money in his pockets, right down to the guy who's just making a few bucks," says Lipuma, himself a former federal prosecutor. "It's frustrating when you have to defend against evidence that has no relevance against your client when the government dumps all this in under a conspiracy."

In the Pops Johnson trial, defense lawyer Cynthia Giachetti effectively conceded all but the murder charges, using her closing argument to attack as liars the four former gang members who testified against her client.

Assistant U.S. Attorney Ronald S. Safer was quick to retort. "Who else do you expect to come in here and testify about these crimes?" Safer asked jurors. "Conspiracies hatched in hell do not have angels as witnesses."

Getting a Few Minnows

In California, gangs typically are not as sophisticated as the Gangster Disciples. "Chicago gangs are set up like organized crime; L.A. gangs are disorganized crime," says Los Angeles gang prosecutor Genelin.

But authorities say California gangs are no less dangerous to the public. In Los Angeles and other communities, authorities believe they have found the perfect tool for dealing with gangs that more closely resemble groups of street punks than La Cosa Nostra.

For nearly a decade, they have been dabbling with public nuisance laws to get civil injunctions forbidding gang members from associating in public and from engaging in other legal activities, such as carrying pagers and cellular phones, which police say are tools of the drug trade.

The California Supreme Court dealt gangs a blow [in 1997] when it rejected a First Amendment challenge to an injunction barring 38 reputed gang members from hanging out in a four-block area of San Jose's Rocksprings neighborhood. Calling the area an "urban war zone" and describing its residents as "prisoners in their own homes," Justice Janice Rogers Brown concluded that something had to give.

"To hold that the liberty of the peaceful, industrious residents of Rocksprings must be forfeited to preserve the illusion of freedom for those whose ill conduct is deleterious to the community as a whole is to ignore half the political promise of the Constitution and the whole of its sense," Brown wrote. . . .

With about a dozen gang injunctions already in place in various areas, officials in Los Angeles obtained the boldest one yet [in the summer of 1997] against 50 members of the 18th Street Gang in the largely crime-ridden and impoverished Pico-Union district.

The square-mile area west of downtown is home to 28,000 people, many of them Latin American immigrants. Police reported a 31 percent reduction in serious crime during September and October, the first two months the injunction was in force.

"It's an enormous drop," Genelin says. "It's one of the toughest areas of the city. It's right in the heart of 18th Street, and the 18th Street Gang is our biggest, baddest street gang.

"A gang can't be a gang if it can't associate in public," he says.

Meeting the Challenges

Because an injunction is a civil proceeding, defendants do not have a right to a government-paid lawyer. But the American Civil Liberties Union [ACLU] has challenged the tactic, claiming in part that it unfairly focuses on minorities.

In addition, says Ramona Ripston, ACLU of Southern California executive director, injunctions don't work and serve only to placate the public. An ACLU analysis of police statistics for another injunction issued in 1993 in the San Fernando Valley showed that crime increased just outside the injunction area, suggesting that gangs merely shifted their activities.

"All it does is move gangs around," Ripston says. "It really doesn't do anything to solve the underlying problem of gangs."

The Illinois Supreme Court in October also took a dim view of a 1992 Chicago city ordinance that allowed police to order that an individual move along if that person is "reasonably believe[d] to be a criminal street gang member loitering in any public place" with at least one other person.

The state supreme court unanimously called the ordinance vague and arbitrary and thus unconstitutional. The justices noted that many of the activities the city hoped to deter through the ordinance already are crimes.

"However, the city cannot empower the police to sweep undesirable persons from the public streets through vague and arbitrary criminal ordinances," wrote Justice John L. Nickels. . . .

Deputy Corporation Counsel Larry Rosenthal says the city has received dozens of calls from other municipalities interested in enacting similar ordinances. He says he expects a broad coalition of government organizations will support Chicago in asking the U.S. Supreme Court to hear the case.

"One of the centerpieces in that petition is going to be how important it is to develop proactive approaches to dealing with gangs," says Rosenthal. "Removing a visibly lawless element from the street is very important."

Regardless of the methods used to take them off the streets and despite complaints from criminal defense lawyers and civil libertarians, state and federal law probably will continue to get tougher on street gangs. That's just too bad for the gangs, says RICO author Blakey.

"No one should shed a tear," Blakey says. "They'll kill anybody. The Mafia is more discreet."

VIEWPOINT

4

> "The War on Youth's buildup began in the late 1980s as . . . 'out-of-control' youths were labeled within a single racialized code word: gangs."

Laws Against Gang Activities Unfairly Target Minority Youth

Ryan Pintado-Vertner and Jeff Chang

In the following viewpoint Ryan Pintado-Vertner and Jeff Chang argue that exaggerated fears of youth crime have led to repressive new antigang laws that criminalize minority youth. The juvenile justice system, to avoid being seen as unnecessarily tough on law-abiding youth, justified its shift in focus from rehabilitation to punishment by calling all juvenile crime committed by minorities "gang activities," they claim. Unfortunately, once such youth are labeled gang members, Pintado-Vertner and Chang contend, establishing a life outside of crime becomes difficult for them. Pintado-Vertner is a member of the *ColorLines* staff, and Chang is managing editor.

As you read, consider the following questions:

1. What facts do the authors cite to support their claim that juvenile crime rates plunged during the 1990s?
2. How have some communities protested the use of gang databases, in the authors' view?
3. According to the author, what are some examples of the "sweep laws" that have proliferated across the country?

Ryan Pintado-Vertner and Jeff Chang, "The War on Youth," *ColorLines*, vol. 2, Winter 1999–2000. Copyright © 2000 by *ColorLines* magazine. Reproduced by permission.

I was as deep as you can get in a gang," says Carlos,[1] a 26-year-old Chicano from the Los Angeles area. Because Carlos lived on the border of rival gang turfs, simply crossing the street meant venturing into enemy territory.

Carlos was smart. He had ambition. But in Carlos' barrio, there were "no community events, no activities," he recalls. "Every time I tried to do something [positive], it was stopped. And the gang was conducive to doing something, not necessarily good, but something."

Three blocks away from his house, at a sunny fourth of July picnic, one of his friends was murdered by the rival gang, his body torn apart by bullets from an AK-47. Carlos began thinking about protecting himself, about what his affiliation really meant.

Soon after, Carlos was arrested for carrying a concealed knife. Tried as an adult, he served six months in county jail. It was his first bid, and it taught him something—something that prosecutors and politicians don't talk about.

"When you're from southern California in a Chicano gang, you could choose to disassociate yourself with your Sureño[2] friends and fend for yourself," he says. But fending for yourself means trying to survive the most dangerous place in the United States alone, with a sell-out reputation, "It ends up being better in the end to join up."

Carlos was stuck. "I remember being told by people in school, 'You are a bright kid, you could do anything you want.' So if I go to prison, I'll be the best that I can be. I'll be in the Syndicate [Mexican Mafia], and be what's called a carnal, a shot-caller," he says. . . .

The Sky Is Falling

During the early 1980s, the government declared a War on Drugs, and a host of repressive new laws took hold in communities of color. Many now question the effects of these laws. Prison expansion and racial profiling have started to come under sustained attack. . . . Even General Barry Mc-Caffrey, the [former] White House drug czar, . . . criticized

1. Names have been changed to ensure anonymity. 2. Sureño, which means "southerner," is a word used by Hispanic gang members as a prefix to their gang name or as an abbreviation that signifies their origin in Southern California.

discriminatory drug sentencing, saying, "It is clear that we cannot arrest our way out of the problem of chronic drug abuse and drug-driven crime."

Yet one core aspect of the War on Drugs remains unchallenged—the targeting of urban youth of color as superpredatory, ultraviolent, drug-infested gangbangers. Here, public opinion has been herded in quite the opposite direction—towards increasing fear.

As so-called Generation Y comes of age some seventy million strong—a cohort projected to swell the under-18 population by as much as 24 percent—criminologists like Northeastern's James Alan Fox, Princeton's John Dilulio, and conservative congressmen like Bill McCollum (R-Fla.) have predicted a juvenile crime wave of tsunami proportions.

"America is a ticking violent crime bomb," warns a widely influential 1996 report, "The State of Violent Crime in America," by the Council on Crime in America (co-chaired by former President [Ronald] Reagan's Secretary of Education, William Bennett). "(R)ates of violent juvenile crime and weapons offenses have been increasing dramatically and by the year 2000 could spiral out of control." In the wake of Columbine,[3] the chorus for punishing juvenile offenders has grown more urgent.

In fact, violent juvenile crime rates have plunged during the 1990s. National homicide arrest rates dropped by forty percent between 1993 and 1997. [In 1999], California reported its lowest juvenile felony arrest rate since 1966. And nationally, juveniles account for just 17 percent of all violent crime arrests. . . .

But the facts don't matter to race-baiting proponents of the War on Youth. The number of young blacks and other people of color is growing much faster than the number of young whites. Fox points to these numbers as an ominous sign. Does he have the sickening hope that racist stereotypes will prove his juvenile crime wave theory or is he just living, as Public Enemy once put it, in fear of a black planet?

Fear of youth and demographic change is not limited to

---

3. On April 20, 1999, Eric Harris and Dylan Klebold gunned down twelve of their fellow students and one teacher at Columbine High School in Colorado.

rightwingers. Despite steeply dropping crime rates, most opinion polls find that adults are pessimistic about today's young people. A . . . study by Public Agenda and the Ad Council found that three-quarters polled viewed children, especially teenagers, in negative terms.

That pessimism is reflected in a major shift in juvenile justice priorities. "We all know that it's a cool thing [for politicians] to be tough on crime. What that translates into for us is being tough on kids," says Lateefah Simon, 22-year-old executive director of the Center for Young Women's Development in San Francisco.

The Costs of Demonizing Minority Youth

The burden of the demonization of youth and youth gangs falls most heavily on minorities, especially young minority males. The names entered on gang databases are almost exclusively those of minorities. Gang membership is so closely associated with minority youth that in some jurisdictions most of the young minority males are considered by the police to be gang members or associates. The close association of gang membership and minority status permits politicians and commentators to "play the race card" indirectly. Public officials may be reluctant to endorse a "war against young minority offenders" or "tougher criminal penalties for young minorities" because of a fear that they will be accused of racism. It is much safer to endorse a "war against gangs" or "tougher criminal penalties for gang members." Gangs become a proxy for race.

Linda S. Beres and Thomas D. Griffith, *Loyola of Los Angeles Law Review*, January 2001.

In 1899, Progressive reformers sought to reverse the horrible conditions and violence that children faced in adult courts and prisons by establishing a separate juvenile justice system. One hundred years later, tough-on-crime politicians seem to have abandoned the idea that youths deserve rehabilitation and concern. Instead, they seem to be embracing the notion that offenders are only worthy of restraint and containment.

This notion is being implemented in state legislatures across the nation. Since 1992, 48 states made their juvenile crime statutes more punitive. Forty-one states made it easier for prosecutors to try juveniles as young as twelve as adults. The number of young adults sentenced under mandatory minimums or jailed in adult prisons has grown dramatically. Forty states have been moving to make it easier to unseal confidential juvenile records.

Across the country, the war has turned against young people. "In Florida, the same number of kids (have been) sent to adult prison on the whim of prosecutors than by the decisions of judges in all the other states combined," says Jason Ziedenburg, policy analyst for the Center on Juvenile and Criminal Justice. "And Florida still has one of the highest crime rates in the nation."

Not surprisingly, youths of color are the overwhelming majority of the War on Youth's casualties. Nationally, although whites make up 68 percent of all juveniles, 63 percent of youths in custody facilities are of color. In California, 86 percent of wards in the California Youth Authority are of color.

"The stark reality is that racism is alive and well in the juvenile justice system," says Mimi Ho, an organizer for Californians for Justice. "They are saying, 'Youth are our future—but not kids of color.'"

Gangs Are a Racialized Code Word

The War on Youth's buildup began in the late 1980s, as jurisdictions increasingly fretted about rising juvenile crime rates and the "out-of-control" youths behind the numbers. In that decade, these "out-of-control" youths were labeled within a single racialized code word: gangs.

But even the Department of Justice finds gang membership difficult to pin down. Gangs are often informal, with unstable memberships. Add the inconsistent data collection criteria in police agencies, and you have Department of Justice estimates of the number of gangs in the U.S. that vary from 4,800 to 23,338.

If the numbers are elusive, the political opportunism is real. In 1988, then-California Governor George Deukmejian signed the Street Terrorism Enforcement and Prevention Act of 1988 (STEP), a model effort that the U.S. Department of Justice called "the most extensive statutory scheme to criminalize gang acts."

The law gave gang-related offenses enhanced punishments, and created new crimes specific to gang activity. Under STEP, gang membership is punishable by up to three years in state prison. Most importantly, STEP wrote into law a process of determining who was a gang member. Today, most major cities and at least 19 states have laws similar to STEP and anti-gang units to enforce them.

In 1987, the Law Enforcement Communication Network and the Los Angeles County Sheriff's Department began developing a large database—the Gang Reporting, Evaluation, and Tracking System (GREAT)—to collect, store, and analyze personal information about suspected gang members. Now simply known as CalGang, the database contains more than 300,000 names and is used by departments across the country. The Justice Department and the FBI also fund national databases.

The Difficulty of Defining Gang Members

Databases indiscriminately criminalize youths, identifying "suspects" before any crime has been committed. Indeed, the definition of a "gang member" is hotly debated. In several cities, the ACLU [American Civil Liberties Union] has filed suits challenging local authorities' definitions of gang membership. Abuses are rampant. Racial profiling, it seems, is most virulent when it comes to youth of color.

In at least five states, wearing baggy FUBU jeans and being related to a gang suspect is enough to meet the "gang member" definition. In Arizona, a tattoo and blue Adidas are sufficient. With so many of the crucial details left up to prejudice, the results are not surprising.

In 1992, Actions for a Better Community (ABC) in Denver began protesting to local police that the city's gang database was criminalizing thousands of innocent youths of color. "Employers could call the gang list to see if a young person was on the list," says Gloria Yellowhorse, an organizer with ABC. A year later, investigations revealed that eight of every ten young people of color in the entire city were listed. Police met with ABC and quietly changed their database protocols.

But minutes away from downtown Denver in suburban

Aurora, any two of the following may still constitute gang membership to the local police: "slang," "clothing of a particular color," "pagers," "hairstyles," or "jewelry." Nearly eighty percent of Aurora's list is African American. The local head of the ACLU was heard to say, "They might as well call it a black list."

But Aurora is no aberration. In Cook County, Illinois, the gang database is two-thirds black. In Orange County, CA, where less than half of young people are of color, 92 percent of those listed in the gang database in 1997 were youths of color. "The 'gang label' has everything to do with race," says John Crew of the California ACLU. "Frankly, we do not believe that this tactic would have spread so widely, and come to be accepted within law enforcement generally, if it was not being applied almost exclusively to people of color."

To Sweep and Destroy

At Coronado Mall in Albuquerque, NM, youths cannot even congregate. Like many shopping centers across the country, Coronado enforces a policy forbidding young people to gather in groups of three or more. Violators are cited for trespassing and banned from the Mall. Their records and photos are then turned over to the police gang unit for possible listing. . . .

Like other War on Youth initiatives, youths of color were the primary targets. "By [one security guard's] count, at least ninety percent of the kids that they brought in were Chicano or Latino," says Robby Rodriguez, the 24-year-old coordinator of the Southwest Organizing Project's campaign against the Mall. "Ninety percent of the youth [hanging out] in the Mall were not Latino."

"[The mall operator's] reasoning was that when young people get together, there's a tendency for them to misbehave and to get into trouble," says Rodriguez. Such is the logic of the sweep—whether public space or private, youth of color have been turned into a generation of suspects.

In the last decade, sweep laws—laws against loitering, anti-truancy ordinances, anti-cruising laws, and curfews—have proliferated across the country. The result? Curfew arrests nationwide doubled between 1988 and 1997. In California, they quadrupled during the same period.

But evidence suggests curfew enforcement is not color blind. According to the Center on Juvenile and Criminal Justice, Ventura County, CA, arrests Latino and black youths at over seven times the rate of whites. In New Orleans, blacks are arrested at 19 times the rate of whites.

A Pervasive Policy

The most famous sweep law was passed in Chicago in 1992—a gang anti-loitering ordinance that made it illegal to stand on the street with any person whom a cop "reasonably believes" to be in a gang. Under the ordinance, 43,000 young Chicagoans were arrested in just two years, the vast majority of them youth of color. Only a tiny fraction of them were actually charged with a crime.

"They were arresting lots of innocent people. It takes police away from the real work, and pushes them to simply sweeping youth off the street," says Jeremy Lahoud, a youth organizer with Chicago's Southwest Youth Collaborative. The law was so broadly dismissive of basic liberties that it was declared unconstitutional by the conservative U.S. Supreme Court [in 1999].

The sweep mentality now pervades even school safety policy. In Oakland, CA, the school board recently voted to spend $1.13 million a year to maintain its own 24-hour-a-day police force. The only board member to vote against the plan said, "When we have to take money from our core educational function, the children suffer."

At Lolita Roibal's high school in Albuquerque, New Mexico, a modern cavalry of police officers patrols on three-wheelers. "Motorized tricycles," she calls them. Students are searched before they enter the dilapidated buildings. "It just feels more like a jail than like a school," says Roibal, an 18-year-old Chicana.

One day, she recalls, two sophomores got into a fight, "so out of nowhere like seven cop cars pull up." As Roibal watched, a cop yelled at a fleeing boy, "Stop, or I'll shoot, you little fucker!"

Shocking? "No, I wasn't shocked," Roibal concedes with a sigh. . . .

The Task of Transformation

Carlos' own road toward transformation began when a friend helped him enroll in community college and a Chicano studies class. Hoping to finish his education and develop his activism, he now calls himself a lucky one. Yet he still lives on the edge, always within the grasp of the system or the streets.

"I think for me I feel like I'm always walking on a tight rope," he says. "I will always forever be in [a gang] because the police have put me down in their records, the courts have put me down in their records, and if things ever get bad for me, it would be really easy for me to jump back into the mold."

"The transformation is possible, but it's really, really big," he says. "I'm still going through it, and I don't know if I'll ever finish it."

"By preventing gangs from flaunting their authority, [anti-loitering] laws establish community authority while combating the perception that gangs have high status."

Antiloitering Laws Reduce Gang Violence

Richard K. Willard

In the following viewpoint, an amicus curiae brief to the U.S. Supreme Court, Richard K. Willard argues in favor of Chicago's 1992 antiloitering law, which made it a crime for gang members or anyone associated with a gang member to stay in one place "with no apparent purpose." Willard maintains that gang-loitering laws reduce violence because they help maintain order. Moreover, he asserts, residents of high-crime areas consider these laws an effective approach to gang violence. On June 10, 1999, the U.S. Supreme Court ruled that the law was unconstitutional. Willard submitted the brief on behalf of the Center for the Community Interest, a national nonprofit organization that seeks to improve civic and community life.

As you read, consider the following questions:

1. According to Willard, what has been the impact of the "quiet revolution" in modern policing theory?
2. What is sometimes the result of "raising the price" of gang activity, in the author's opinion?
3. In the author's view, what are the most successful anti-gang programs?

Richard K. Willard, *amicas curiae brief*, submitted to the U.S. Supreme Court, June 19, 1998, on behalf of the Center for Community Interest, *City of Chicago, Illinois, v. Jesus Morales et al.*

Chicago is not alone in seeking to resist the devastating effects of gang violence. Having witnessed the failure of more traditional policing methods, many other threatened localities—from Los Angeles to Washington, D.C.—have reacted by passing a variety of innovative laws, which range from curfew measures to anti-loitering statutes to court injunctions against specific gang members. All of these measures emphasize prevention and deterrence strategies over increased criminal sanctions. In order to meet the particular challenges of increased gang violence, communities have also strongly supported constrained expansions of police discretion, to help communities reassert their own law-abiding norms.

Residents of high-crime communities are much more likely to support gang-loitering ordinances, curfews, and other order-maintenance policies, which they perceive to be appropriately moderate yet effective devices for reducing crime. Communities have implemented these policies in various ways, tailored to their particular needs, and depending on the pervasiveness of the problem.

Modern Policing Theory

Just as community disorder engenders increasing disorder and crime, reinforcement of [existing] community law-abiding norms engenders increasing social order and prevents more serious crime. Modern policing theory has undergone a "quiet revolution" to learn that, in cooperation with community efforts, enforcing community public order norms is one of the most effective means of combating all levels of crime. By focusing on order maintenance and prevention, advocating a more visible presence in policed areas, and basing its legitimacy on the consent of policed populations, police can most effectively prevent the occurrence of more serious crime.

New York City's experience confirms this. Today, that city has much less crime than it did five years ago. From 1993 to 1996, the murder rate dropped by 40 percent, robberies dropped by 30 percent, and burglary dropped by more than 25 percent, more than double the national average.

These drops are not the result of increased police resources, but rather more effectively applied resources. While New York has not increased its law enforcement expenditures substantially more than other cities, since 1993, the city began to focus intensively on "public order" offenses, including vandalism, aggressive panhandling, public drunkenness, unlicensed vending, public urination, and prostitution. This focus on order maintenance is credited for much of the crime reduction.

A Less Abusive Policing Strategy

For those concerned about police abuse, a policing strategy that directs police to warn loiterers to move on before they are subject to arrest and search fares strikingly well when considered in terms of the magnitude of the authority that it confers on the police. To be sure, groups of loiterers containing no one with a gang or drug affiliation may occasionally be inappropriately or unfairly ordered to disperse, but that inconvenience pales in comparison to being detained, searched, ticketed, or even arrested. Even more important, to the extent that the police devote their limited resources to dispersal of loiterers, the use of much harsher sanctions will decrease.

Lawrence Rosenthal, *Journal of Criminal Law & Criminology*, Fall 2000.

Anti-loitering ordinances implement community-driven order maintenance policing citywide—appropriate to the extreme pervasiveness of Chicago's gang problem—but on a neighborhood scale. Preservation of neighborhood commons is essential to ensuring healthy and vital cities.

The Problem with Conventional Strategies

Gang loitering works to increase disorder. Order-maintenance policing strikes a reasonable intermediate balance between harsh criminal penalties and inaction. Conventional suppression strategies are ineffective in gang-threatened communities. Where gang activity is prevalent, individuals are more likely to act in an aggressive manner in order to conform to gang norms of behavior. When numerous youths act according to these skewed norms, more are likely to turn to crime: Widespread adoption of aggressive mannerisms sends skewed signals about public attitudes toward gang membership and creates barriers to mainstream law-abiding society, which strongly disfavors aggression.

Accordingly, policies that "raise the price" of gang activity can sometimes function at cross-purposes. If juveniles value willingness to break the law, delinquency may be seen as "status-enhancing." As penalties grow more severe, law-breaking gives increasing status. More severe punishments may also provoke unintended racist accusation, if community minorities view harsher penalties as unfairly applied to their particular groups. Thus, any strategy dependent on harsh penalties may in fact be "at war with itself."

Anti-Loitering Laws Are Effective

Strategies that instead attack public signals to juveniles' peers about the value of gang criminality are more effective. Gang anti-loitering laws do this, for example, by "authorizing police to disperse known gang members when they congregate in public places," or by "directly prohibiting individuals from displaying gang allegiance through distinctive gestures or clothing." By preventing gangs from flaunting their authority, such laws establish community authority while combating the perception that gangs have high status. As that perception weakens, so does the pressure to join gangs that youths might otherwise perceive.

Such strategies also positively influence law-abiding adults. Gang-loitering laws augment law-abiders' confidence so that they can oppose gangs. When public deterrence predominates, individuals are much less likely to perceive that criminality is widespread and much more likely to see private precautions as worthwhile. When the community as a whole is again able to express its condemnation, gang influence quickly wanes.

The most successful anti-gang programs combine effective gang suppression programs with targeted community aid efforts: increased social services, job placement, and crisis intervention. Civil gang abatement, together with other government and community-based efforts, has reduced crime and visibly improved the neighborhood's quality of life.

Chicago has also implemented alternative community aid programs. Since 1992, for example, the Gang Violence Reduction Project has targeted Little Village to serve as a model gang violence reduction program.

The program coordinates increased levels of social services—the carrot—in conjunction with focused suppression strategies—the stick. The result has been a lower level of serious gang violence among the targeted gangs than among comparable gangs in the area. The project also noted improvement in residents' perceptions of gang crime and police effectiveness in dealing with it. Chicago's anti-loitering ordinance is the necessary "stick" of an effective gang violence reduction equation.

"Police have a tendency to enforce the law against groups they disfavor and this often means members of minority groups."

Antiloitering Laws Unfairly Target Minorities

Dorothy Roberts

Antiloitering laws do not protect minority communities from gang violence, writes Dorothy Roberts in the following viewpoint. In fact, she argues, these statutes, which allow police to arrest individuals suspected of being gang members even if they are simply talking on the street, unfairly target minorities in communities the laws are designed to protect. Because law enforcement officials think most gang members are members of minority groups, they use race to distinguish gang members from non–gang members. When determining who should disperse under gang-loitering laws, therefore, the police are disproportionately targeting minorities. Roberts, a professor at Northwestern University School of Law, is author of *Killing the Black Body: Race, Reproduction, and Meaning of Liberty.*

As you read, consider the following questions:

1. What burden should be placed on those who use racial politics to defend state incursion on inner-city residents' freedoms, in the author's view?
2. According to Roberts, why was it presumptuous to claim that the inner-city residents of Chicago had voluntarily relinquished their civil liberties in exchange for safer streets?

Dorothy Roberts, "It's All About Race: Vague Anti-Loitering Laws Target Minorities," *Chicago Tribune*, June 18, 1999, p. 31. Copyright © 1999 by Tribune Media Services, Inc. All rights reserved. Reproduced by permission of the author.

The Supreme Court's decision [in 1999] concluding that Chicago's gang-loitering ordinance is unconstitutionally vague will not put an end to the matter. Justice Sandra Day O'Connor suggested several ways the city might rewrite the law to cure its constitutional defects, and Mayor [Richard M.] Daley has vowed to produce a new version.[1] . . . Although the justices did not find race discrimination, issues of race have been at the center of the debate surrounding the liotering law.

According to the Illinois ACLU [American Civil Liberties Union], most of the 42,000 people arrested for loitering were black or Latino residents of inner-city neighborhoods. This is not surprising: Chicago Police Department officials identify nearly all of the city's street gangs as belonging to these groups. What is surprising is that supporters and opponents of the ordinance pointed to race in their constitutional arguments.

Using the Law to Target Minorities

Racism is a motivating concern underlying the constitutional objections to vague loitering laws like the Chicago ordinance. Broadly worded statutes permit police to haul off the streets people who look suspicious even though they have committed no criminal conduct. Without clear guidelines, police have a tendency to enforce the law against groups they disfavor and this often means members of minority groups.

Chicago's ordinance gave police an especially wide net to trap groups that included a suspected gang member standing in any public place "with no apparent purpose." According to the city's brief in the Supreme Court, police were supposed to arrest "visibly lawless" people—people who look like criminals even when they are doing no more than standing still. How do police officers distinguish between "visibly lawless" people and law-abiding ones apart from their criminal conduct?

Police officers routinely use racial profiling to make this determination; they consider an individual's race in their decision to stop and detain him. Evidence is mounting, for ex-

1. Chicago's amended ordinance became effective in 2000.

ample, that motorists across the country are stopped on the basis of race for minor traffic violations, commonly known as "driving while black." The gang-loitering ordinance codified a police practice that many regard as racial harassment, backing it up with arrest, conviction and incarceration.

Turning the Race Argument Around

Ironically, race is also at the center of the most powerful argument in favor of upholding the ordinance or a narrower version of it. Some of the law's defenders argue that black support for the law demonstrates its efficacy at protecting inner-city communities from crime and outweighs concerns about the violations of citizens' liberties. A brief filed in the Supreme Court on behalf of 20 neighborhood organizations claimed that the law had the overwhelming support of inner-city residents who experienced gang violence and intimidation on a daily basis.

Anti-Loitering Laws Fuel Racial Tension

If anti-loitering laws were effective and did in fact reduce the crime rate, then every area with gang problems would have them in effect. If the laws worked so well, then of course there would be few to oppose them. Unfortunately, this seemingly quick fix is not a fix at all; it just fuels underlying racial issues and makes discrimination legal. In the past, these types of laws have been imposed upon minorities for the sole purpose of keeping them in check and the laws were blatantly used as a basis of discrimination.

Heather Slater, *OpinionEditorials.com*, April 18, 2003.

In a series of academic articles, University of Chicago law professors Tracey Meares and Dan Kahan argued that constitutional standards like that used by the court to invalidate the loitering law have outlived their utility and should be replaced by a new criminal procedure regime that is less hostile to police discretion. Rules that curb that discretion, they contend, used to protect black citizens from racist law-enforcement practices; now they prevent black citizens from protecting themselves from gang violence.

Is the disproportionate arrest of minorities under the ordinance evidence of racial discrimination, or evidence that the Chicago Police Department is finally starting to protect the city's minority communities from the internal threat of gangs? Given persistent evidence of racial bias in arrests and the political vulnerability of racial minorities, those who use racial politics to defend state incursion on inner-city residents' freedoms should bear a heavy burden of proof. They have failed to make their case.

A Presumptuous Claim

To begin with, there is no evidence that most blacks in Chicago endorse the ordinance. We have no reliable way of determining inner-city residents' opinions about the law, and most of their representatives—members of the City Council, the NAACP [National Association for the Advancement of Colored People] and other civic organizations, and grassroots groups such as the Chicago Alliance for Neighborhood Safety—opposed it. A study published [in 1999] shows that blacks in Chicago and nationwide are more wary of police than are whites. . . . Police killings of two unarmed black motorists, LaTanya Haggerty and Robert Russ, and the federal inquiry into the 1996 killing of Emmett Blanton Jr. will only intensify this mistrust.

Moreover, the ordinance was passed by the predominantly white Chicago City Council, not an inner-city political body. The people who will bear the burden of the law's restrictions on freedom and who are the most subject to arrest do not control the city's political processes or police department policies. It is therefore highly presumptuous to claim that inner-city residents have voluntarily relinquished their civil liberties in exchange for safer streets.

Black Americans should have greater say in crime control strategies deployed in their communities. This goal requires that we strengthen constitutional safeguards against race-based police abuse, not weaken or maneuver around them.

"Law enforcement agencies have welcomed anti-gang injunctions as the appropriate solution for an urban problem that has grown out of control."

Injunctions Restricting Gang Activities Reduce Gang Violence

Gregory S. Walston

In the following viewpoint Gregory S. Walston, former deputy attorney general of California, argues that because gangs have become a public nuisance, communities have the right to seek injunctions to prevent gang members from congregating and intimidating local residents. Gang members have no constitutionally protected right to subject law-abiding citizens to intimidation and violence, Walston claims. Moreover, injunctions that prohibit specific conduct are consitutional, he maintains.

As you read, consider the following questions:

1. According to one study cited by Walston, what was the ratio of gang members to police officers in Los Angeles County?
2. Why is the Supreme Court's decision in *Chicago v. Morales* not controlling on the issue of the constitutionality of antigang injunctions, in the author's view?
3. In Walston's opinion, what would happen to the U.S Constitution if egregious acts of concerted lawlessness and violence were constitutionally protected activities?

Gregory S. Walston, "Taking the Constitution at Its Word: A Defense of the Use of Anti-Gang Injunctions," *University of Miami Law Review*, vol. 54, October 1999. Copyright © 1999 by the *University of Miami Law Review*. Reproduced by permission.

Communities throughout America are beset by increasing problems of gang violence. Once confined to inner cities, gang activities have erupted to threaten virtually all neighborhoods in America, turning formerly unfathomed acts of violence into familiar news stories. Public schools have erupted into war zones; individuals have been slain merely for wearing the wrong color; entire communities have become virtual hostages because they live in a neighborhood that is the occupied "turf" of a criminal street gang.

Searching for Solutions

The rising problem of gang violence has overwhelmed conventional law enforcement techniques. District Attorneys cannot combat criminal street gangs effectively because gang members intimidate potential witnesses into turning a blind eye to the criminal activities of the street gang. One study has indicated that Los Angeles County, alone, had 150,000 gang members in 1992. Another study has demonstrated that gang members outnumbered police officers at a ratio of six to one in Los Angeles County. In short, in the midst of overwhelming lawlessness and violence, conventional law enforcement techniques are rendered ineffective in combating modern street gangs.

Law enforcement agencies have been left with no choice but to search for more effective gang-prevention techniques. The most effective of these new techniques is perhaps the most novel—enjoining the gang as a public nuisance. Although this practice was born in Los Angeles, it first attracted notoriety when it was employed in a San Jose, California, neighborhood known as "Rocksprings," an area in which gang activity had reached a level of grim intensity. Members of the Varrio Sureno Treces gang literally took over Rocksprings, subjecting local residents to virtual mob rule.

Residents of Rocksprings became prisoners in their own homes. Their friends and family refused to visit. They remained indoors, especially at night, and they did not allow their children to play outside. A little girl who was allowed to play outside was threatened by Varrio Sureno Treces members, who told her they would cut out her tongue if she ever cooperated with the authorities.

Rocksprings residents were overwhelmed by the problems created by gangs. As a result, the San Jose City Attorney sought an injunction against the activities of the Varrio Sureno Treces gang on grounds that the gang was a public nuisance. The trial court agreed with the City Attorney, and issued the injunction. The injunction prohibited gang members from (1) congregating with other Varrio Sureno Treces members within Rocksprings; (2) trespassing or defacing the property of Rocksprings residents; and (3) harassing, intimidating, and annoying local residents of Rocksprings.

Meeting Constitutional Challenges

Upon appeal of the injunction by the Varrio Sureno Treces members, the California Court of Appeal ruled that the "harassing, intimidating and annoying" language of the injunction was unconstitutionally vague and overbroad and that the prohibition of the gang members' congregating in Rocksprings violated their First Amendment right to free association. The appellate court struck down fifteen of the twenty-four provisions of the injunction, including the prohibition of Varrio Sureno Treces members from congregating and the prohibition of gang harassment, intimidation, and annoyance of local residents.

The City Attorney successfully sought review by the California Supreme Court. The California Supreme Court, in *People ex rel. Gallo v. Acuna* overturned the appellate decision. Underscoring the critical gang problems in Rocksprings and throughout America, the California Supreme Court held that the anti-gang injunction was neither vague nor overbroad because its terms were reasonably clear in the context of the Varrio Sureno Treces gang. The Court also held that the anti-gang injunction did not violate the free association rights of the Varrio Sureno Treces members because there is no cognizable First Amendment right to free association implicated by membership in a criminal street gang.

Although the Varrio Sureno Treces members sought certiorari by the United States Supreme Court, the writ was denied. Thus, in California, anti-gang injunctions have become an established law enforcement tool. In fact, California law enforcement agencies have welcomed anti-gang injunctions

Behavior That Gang Injunctions Often Prohibit

- Standing, sitting, walking, driving, bicycling, gathering or appearing anywhere in public view with any other suspected gang member. . . .
- Using or being under the influence of illegal drugs.
- Drinking or possessing alcoholic beverages; being under the influence of alcohol; knowingly remaining in the presence of anyone possessing an open container of an alcoholic beverage.
- Possessing any firearms, including pellet or BB guns, knives, sharpened screwdrivers, sticks, rocks and bottles. Having baseball bats and golf clubs without a legitimate purpose also is prohibited.
- Fighting in public streets, alleys or on public or private property.
- Possessing marker pens, spray paint cans, nails, razor blades, or other sharp objects capable of defacing private or public property.
- Being present on any property not open to the general public except with prior written consent of the owner or in the presence and with the consent of the owner or the owner's representative.
- In any manner confronting, intimidating, annoying, harassing, threatening, challenging, provoking, assaulting or battering any residents, patrons or visitors to the targeted areas.
- Possessing, without a legitimate purpose, rocks, slim jims, spark plugs, any part of the spark plug, or any other device capable of being used to break into locked vehicles.
- Using physical gestures or symbols known as hand signs or other forms of communication that refer to the gangs.
- Wearing clothes or accessories that bear the name, initials, letters, numbers or other symbols of the gang.
- Making or causing loud noise of any kind, including yelling or loud music, at any time of day or night.

Scott Marshall, *North (San Diego) County Times*, August 12, 2001.

as the appropriate solution for an urban problem that has grown out of control. The California Legislature has amended the California Street Terrorism Enforcement and Prevention Act to permit the California Attorney General to maintain an action against enjoined street gangs for damages.

Support for anti-gang injunctions in California has been fueled by its success as a weapon to combat gang activity.

Examining the Opposition

Not all, however, share these sentiments. Many commentators have criticized the California Supreme Court's decision in *Acuna*. These critics call the use of injunctive relief against gangs violative of the gang members' First Amendment rights to free association and free speech, as well as the right to due process of law. The most impassioned criticism of the *Acuna* injunction comes from Justice [Stanley] Mosk, the lone dissenter in *Acuna*. Justice Mosk apparently viewed the *Acuna* injunction as a racially-discriminatory deprivation of the rights of Latinos to free association under the First Amendment. Justice Mosk complained that the injunction against the Varrio Sureno Treces gang "deprives a number of simple rights to a group of Latino youths." Pointing to Benjamin Franklin's admonition that "they that can give up essential liberty to obtain a little temporary safety deserve neither liberty nor safety," Justice Mosk concluded, inter alia, that the portions of the injunction limiting the gang's right to associate with one another should be stricken.

Arguments that anti-gang injunctions are unconstitutional have been fueled recently by the United States Supreme Court decision in *City of Chicago v. Morales*. In *Morales*, the Supreme Court determined the constitutionality of a "gang loitering" ordinance. The Chicago ordinance prohibited individuals from loitering with gang members. The ordinance defined "gang member" as any individual a police officer reasonably believes to be in a gang. The ordinance defined "loitering" as "remaining in one place with no apparent purpose."

The court struck down the ordinance in a plurality opinion finding the definition of loitering unconstitutionally vague because neither citizens nor police officers could discern what constituted "remaining in one place with no apparent purpose." The Court concluded that this vagueness did not provide insufficient notice of the prohibited conduct and consequentially allowed for arbitrary enforcement by the police.

Answering the Critics

Morales, however, is not controlling on the issue of the constitutionality of anti-gang injunctions. Anti-gang injunctions, unlike the gang loitering ordinance at issue in *Morales*, unambiguously define specific types of prohibited conduct. The *Morales* Court recognized the narrow scope of its holding, stating expressly that the decision was limited to the specific ambiguities in the Chicago ordinance. Justice O'-Connor, in a concurring opinion, wrote:

> It is important to courts and legislatures alike that we characterize more clearly the narrow scope of today's holding. As the ordinance comes to this Court, it is unconstitutionally vague. Nevertheless, there remain open to Chicago reasonable alternatives to combat the very real threat posed by gang intimidation and violence. For example, the Court properly and expressly distinguishes the ordinance from laws that require loiterers to have a "harmful purpose," from laws that target only gang members, and from laws that incorporate limits on the area and manner in which the laws may be enforced. In addition the ordinance here is unlike a law that "directly prohibits" the "'presence of a large collection of obviously brazen, insistent and lawless gang members and hangers on in the public ways'" that "'intimidates residents.'"

Thus, the Supreme Court's decision in *Morales* does not implicate the constitutionality of anti-gang injunctions. More direct attacks on the constitutionality of anti-gang injunctions, such as Justice Mosk's, also ring hollow. At the outset, Justice Mosk's characterization of anti-gang injunctions as a deprivation of Latino rights diverts the issue. Anti-gang injunctions do not implicate race. They target all gang-related activities, irrespective of the gang's racial composition. Thus, Justice Mosk's attempt to cast injunctions into a light of racial animus is utterly misguided.

Justice Mosk's quotation of Benjamin Franklin also fails to support the conclusion that the concerted lawlessness of street gangs is protected by the Constitution. Although Justice Mosk may think the residents of Rocksprings "deserve neither safety nor liberty" because they "seek a little safety" from the Varrio Sureno Treces gang, his view is not legally supported. Egregious acts of concerted lawlessness and violence are not constitutionally protected activities. To hold otherwise would effectively turn the Constitution on its head by destroying the ability of the government to govern and rendering constitutionally protected liberty a perpetuum of anarchy.

The California Supreme Court correctly held that gang activities may be enjoined as public nuisances. The activities of street gangs rely on territorial control carried out by violence and threats of violence. It is well established and indeed necessary, that an individual who commits an act of violence may be prosecuted without constitutional implication.

Anti-gang injunctions are the appropriate reconciliation of the relevant competing interests. The civil liberties of the gang members are at stake, the public safety and welfare interests of the community are threatened, and the rights of the common citizen are at risk. Because it is unreasonable to expect the common citizen to constantly be subjected to the inherent intimidation and violence of criminal street gangs, anti-gang injunctions present the proper solution for resolving these conflicting interests.

"More than half of those convicted committed crimes in the injunctions' target neighborhoods, indicating that gang members neither ended their criminal acts nor moved away."

Injunctions Restricting Gang Activities Alone Are Ineffective

Wendy Thomas Russell

Injunctions that prohibit specific gang activities such as associating in public have gained popularity nationwide, but alone they fail to reduce gang-related crime, claims Wendy Thomas Russell in the following viewpoint. Russell is a staff writer for the *Long Beach Press-Telegram*, which studied the impact of antigang injunctions on Long Beach's gang-ridden communities. The study found that injunctions not only did not prevent gang members from committing crimes, innocent victims continued to die as a result of gang warfare. According to Russell, law enforcement authorities and citizens alike are not convinced injunctions are an effective way to reduce gang violence in American communities.

As you read, consider the following questions:
1. In Russell's view, what do prosecutors use to draft injunctions that target specific gang members?
2. According to Russell, what do the experts say is difficult about assessing the effectiveness of gang injunctions?
3. In the author's opinion, why did gang injunctions work better in the early years of their use?

Wendy Thomas Russell, "Do Gang Injunctions Work?" *Long Beach Press-Telegram*, November 15, 2003. Copyright © 2003 by *Long Beach Press-Telegram*, Los Angeles Newspaper Group. Reproduced by permission of the author.

Gang injunctions, an increasingly popular but controversial method of combating street gangs in cities across the country, have failed to persuade most of the targeted gang members in Long Beach to halt their criminal behavior, according to a study by the [*Long Beach*] *Press-Telegram*.

The injunctions are court orders intended to prohibit named members of gangs from engaging in a litany of criminal and nuisance behavior within specific neighborhoods.

"This is the beginning of disarmament," City Prosecutor Tom Reeves declared [in 2001 when], announcing an injunction against the East Side Longos, the city's third gang injunction and the first prepared by Reeves.

"We will take the guns out of the hands of the East Side Longos first . . . and we will have peace on our streets," Reeves said.

The Study Results

Yet, nearly 80 percent of the gang members named in that injunction, and in a 1997 order against members of the West Coast Crips, have been convicted of at least one crime since the injunctions were imposed, the *Press-Telegram* found.

More than half of those convicted committed crimes in the injunctions' target neighborhoods, indicating that gang members neither ended their criminal acts nor moved away after being served with court orders to do so.

The newspaper also found:

- The issuing of injunctions in the two areas studied was not always followed by a reduction in violent crime. While the West Coast Crips area in West Long Beach experienced a drop in crime the first year after an injunction was imposed, the East Side Longos area in Central Long Beach saw a marked increase in both aggravated assaults and robberies during the corresponding period.

- Gang injunctions aren't enforced uniformly. Long Beach police detectives use discretion when deciding whether to make arrests for injunction violations, and some detectives prefer to use the court orders as negotiating tools to gain information on the streets, rather than as grounds for arrest.

- Many residents in injunction areas report improvements in their neighborhoods but say they cannot credit injunctions alone, because other neighborhood projects and crime-fighting programs began around the same time.

Reeves, who has now written two of Long Beach's four injunctions, says he is disappointed with the findings, but not alarmed.

"The fact that (gang members) continue to offend does not surprise me because it's exactly that kind of conduct that the injunction is trying to stop," he says. "Do I think the injunction is going to stop them? No . . . It's not the answer; it's a tool."

How Injunctions Work

Injunctions, which originated [a little over] two decades ago in East Los Angeles, prohibit illegal activities, such as drinking in public, vandalizing property and selling drugs, as well as certain legal activities, such as using hand signs and gathering in public with other gang members.

Prosecutors draft injunctions to target specific gang members, using police reports and court records to prove a person's gang membership and history. Once a judge issues a court order, those caught in violation can be charged with contempt of court, a misdemeanor carrying a first-time sentence of a few days in jail and a fine.

The American Civil Liberties Union [ACLU] has long criticized injunctions for prohibiting people from engaging in otherwise legal activities. Some critics say the injunctions are unfair, inaccurate and even racist.

Yet injunctions have gained widespread popularity in big cities across the country. Long Beach, home to more than 6,000 gang members, has four injunctions in place: against the West Side Longos (1995), the West Coast Crips (1997), the East Side Longos (2001) and the Insane Crips (2003). A fifth injunction, which will again target the West Side Longos, is on the way.

Los Angeles, with an estimated 800 gangs and 56,000 gang members, has implemented 17 injunctions. The first to gain national attention, against the Playboy Gangster Crips in 1987, proved politically popular. The man who issued it, Los Angeles City Attorney James Hahn, is now the city's mayor. Police and prosecutors in Los Angeles and Long Beach say the injunctions are effective tools for battling violent crime, and that their ability to curb nuisance activity has been felt countywide. But the opinions are based largely on anecdotal evidence. Despite the nation's two decades of experience, experts say they know relatively little about the injunctions' potency, cost-effectiveness or long-term impacts.

A Lack of Data

"Prosecutors aren't doing community surveys," says Malcolm Klein, a professor emeritus of criminology at the University of Southern California. "They aren't doing careful criminal analysis of arrest records, not comparing before and after crime rates. . . . Accountability is very low."

Long Beach Police Chief Anthony Batts says he supports the use of gang injunctions, but even he is unconvinced that they are accomplishing all they should.

"I can't sit here and tell you that I'm 100 percent behind it or 100 percent not behind it until I sit down and look at the results and see if it's making an impact or not," he says.

To measure the impact, the *Press-Telegram* analyzed the criminal records of 42 gang members, whose names appeared in a pair of gang injunctions, and conducted numerous interviews with police, residents and gang experts about their observations and experiences.

Of Long Beach's four injunctions, the latest, against the Insane Crips gang, was too recent to analyze results. And crime data for most people cited in the first injunction, against the West Side Longos, could not be located.

So the *Press-Telegram* analyzed the second and third injunctions, against the West Coast Crips and the East Side Longos.

Examining Criminal History

The analysis found that of 19 West Coast Crips whose criminal histories could be tracked, 15, or 79 percent, have been convicted of crimes since the injunction took effect. Eight of the 15, or 53 percent, have been convicted of crimes committed in the target area. (The injunction covered 21 people, but records for two of them could not be found.)

Of the 23 men named in the East Side Longos injunction, three were imprisoned at the time and have yet to be released, so the injunction has not affected them at all. Of the remaining 20, 16, or 80 percent, have committed offenses since the injunction. Eleven of those offenders, 73 percent, did so in the target area.

[As of November 2003], 10 of the men named in the two injunctions are serving state prison terms, four have been . . . released from prison, and three are in the custody of the Los Angeles Sheriff's Department, awaiting trial. Many of the others are on probation or parole. Most of those whose whereabouts are known still live in Long Beach.

Looking for a Better Solution

Injunctions are not enough to keep gangs from tearing up a community, said William "Blinky" Rodriguez, whose 16-year-old son was shot and killed in 1990 in a drive-by attack in Sylmar [California]. A member of the Victory Outreach Ministries, Rodriguez managed to forgive the killers of his son, and has dedicated his life to bringing peace among rival gangs.

"Injunctions sometimes work up to a point, but it can't just be suppression; there's got to be a balanced approach," said Rodriguez, who heads a gang-counseling center in the San Fernando Valley. "This is a Band-Aid solution."

Joseph Trevino, *LA Weekly*, May 25–31, 2001.

Of the 31 named gang members who were convicted of crimes since the injunctions, seven have been convicted of violating the injunction at least once. The rest have been convicted of other crimes, ranging from traffic offenses to drug sales to robbery.

That gang members tend to stick close to their territory, with or without an injunction, makes sense to gang experts.

"Most gangs, as you well know, have their own turf," says Robert Walker, a former law enforcement officer and expert witness on gangs who runs a Web site called "Gangs or Us" from his home in South Carolina. "An injunction, or a court order of any sort, is not going to cause them to leave the area where they feel safe."

The Violence Continues

Unfortunately, that feeling of safety isn't shared by other residents of the injunctions' targeted neighborhoods. In the East Side Longos area, violence continues to claim a seemingly endless stream of innocent victims:

- On Oct. 19, [2003], Cambodian-born Marine Lance Cpl. Sok Khak Ung, just back from the war in Iraq, was gunned down, while barbecuing at his father's home near Seventh Street and Orange Avenue, the epicenter of East Side Longos territory. A friend, Vouthy Tho, also was killed.

  Ung had earned a Purple Heart in Iraq and aided in the rescue of Army Pfc. Jessica Lynch. Police say his killer may have been a gang member.

- Five days earlier and just eight blocks away, Francis Joel Rivers, a 26-year-old father who struggled with multiple sclerosis, was murdered in a drive-by shooting on the front lawn of a home in the 1400 block of Cerritos Avenue. The shooting is believed to have been gang-related, but police say Rivers was not a gang member.

- And in June [2003], a schoolteacher named Patricia Anne Miller was killed and her son wounded as they drove to a coin laundry near 15th Street and Alamitos Avenue. Miller's suspected killer, Melvin James Jones, is alleged to be a member of a predominantly Cambodian gang. He was arrested and is now awaiting trial.

In the first full year after the East Side Longos injunction took effect, most types of violent crime rose. The number of robberies grew 25 percent, to 291 in 2002 from 218 in 2001. Aggravated assaults rose 6 percent, to 341 from 319. The number of rapes went to 19 from 18, and the number of murders stayed the same: 11.

Explaining Crime Statistics

Still, crime statistics are fallible, affected by any number of factors that contribute to the ebb and flow of criminal activity.

Jeffrey Grogger, a professor in UCLA's [University of California, at Los Angeles'] Department of Policy Studies, published the county's best-known and oft-quoted study on the effectiveness of gang injunctions. He says the crime statistics in the East Side Longos area do not necessarily mean the injunction has failed to reduce violent crime.

"It's possible, it's conceivable, that despite the increase that you observe in Long Beach, crime would have been higher anyway if the injunction would not have been imposed," he says.

Reeves agrees.

"How many assaults didn't happen?" he asks. "How many batteries didn't happen? It's hard to gauge, and there are so many, many ingredients that go into crime statistics."

Grogger's study, which looked at 14 gang injunctions implemented in Los Angeles, Pasadena and Long Beach between 1993 and 1998, determined that injunctions lowered violent crime by an average of 5 percent to 10 percent in the year after they were implemented.

Indeed, the West Coast Crips injunction, which was part of Grogger's study, was followed by a dip in violent crime during that time period. In 1997, there was one murder, one rape, 18 robberies and 33 aggravated assaults. In 1998, there were no murders, one rape, eight robberies and 31 aggravated assaults.

Based on anecdotal evidence, Reeves says he strongly believes the injunctions have led to a drop in nuisance activities, such as vandalism and drinking in public.

"I don't see as many complaints about gang bangers congregating," he says. "I see a reduction in the amount of tagging incidents."

Feeling Safer

Some residents interviewed say they, too, have noticed changes in their neighborhoods since the injunctions took effect.

Michelle Arend-Ekhoff, a teacher who lives at Eighth Street and Orange Avenue, in East Side Longos territory, says things were worse [in 2001], before the injunction was introduced.

"There was a lot of congregation of gang members," she says. "I see a lot less of that, and I see a lot less graffiti."

Westside residents say the West Coast Crips injunction

156

seemed to make their area safer, too.

"Before they put this gang injunction in, you wouldn't find someone in Silverado Park at night," says John Cross, past president of the West Long Beach Association. "Now, you see people playing basketball, picnicking, playing."

An Alternative Explanation

But most residents and activists say a number of factors played into those neighborhood improvements.

Marcia Rhone, a community policing coordinator for the Long Beach Police Department [LBPD], says gang activity was attacked on a number of fronts at the time, and that injunctions were one important piece.

"You needed the injunction," she says. "You needed nuisance abatement. You needed community policing teams. You needed the residents themselves. Those four working together made a big difference."

Arend-Ekhoff says she and her neighbors had something to do with the safer streets in her neighborhood, too. They founded "Neighborhoods Organized for a Safer Environment," for example, to clean up the area and improve property values.

"I can't necessarily credit (all the improvements) to the injunction," she says.

Andy Whallon, manager of the El Capitan Condominiums Complex, on Santa Fe Avenue in West Long Beach, says residents there saw lots of gang activity in the 1990s, and the 1997 injunction did almost nothing to stop it.

In 2000, police received 710 service calls from the building, almost two a day, Whallon says.

Things have changed dramatically at the El Capitan since then, he says, but it was his own security measures, installing lights in the alley, hiring a security guard and spending more hours on site, that did the trick. [In 2002], the complex logged 336 calls for service, he says.

Part of the difficulty in assessing the effectiveness of gang injunctions is that their success tends to shift over time and vary from location to location, some experts say.

There are neighborhoods in Los Angeles where gang members have all but disappeared as a result of injunctions,

Grogger says. The very act of serving the court orders, putting gangsters on notice that they were being watched, was enough to win instant results.

But other areas, Grogger says, are more impervious to change.

"The response to these gang injunctions seems to be as heterogeneous as the areas where they're imposed."

The Nature of Gang Boundaries

LBPD Cmdr. William Blair agrees, adding that the way gangs operate affects how the injunctions will work against them.

In Long Beach, where gangs tend to be more racial than territorial, it's more difficult to keep track of them, Blair says, and more difficult to catch them in the target areas.

Unlike in Los Angeles, where gangs are often rigidly tied to certain blocks, local gang members and their families often live in rental apartments, and they tend to move frequently, Blair says. Also, the neighborhoods are some of the most racially diverse in the country, so territorial boundaries stay relatively porous.

"It's more transient," Blair says of the gang population. "Quite honestly, we find that they are all over the place."

About two dozen gang detectives are on Long Beach's streets on any given night, Blair says. They are the only officers trained to enforce the injunctions. With more than 40 gangs, 6,000 gang members and 50 square miles to cover, he says, the odds of catching someone violating an injunction are stacked against the officers.

Still, Blair says, it happens, and he believes strongly that, overall, injunctions are a positive force in communities.

Enforcing Injunctions

So far, four members of the East Side Longos and three members of the West Coast Crips have been convicted of contempt of court for violating an injunction.

Others on the injunction lists have been caught but charged with more serious crimes, rendering a contempt-of-court allegation meaningless.

And some, police detectives acknowledge, are caught but

not arrested. Detectives say they get more mileage from the gang injunctions by using them as a negotiating tool to gain information on the streets. Such information can help officers connect gang members to each other, find out what battles are heating up and even solve murders, they say.

That concept slightly rankles Cheryl Maxson, an associate professor in the Department of Criminology, Law and Society at UC [University of California] Irvine. She says it's hard enough to decipher how injunctions perform without having enforcement vary from one jurisdiction to the next.

"If an injunction is not strongly implemented," she says, "then, logically, you have a hard time associating outcomes with that intervention."

Whether gang injunctions have lost some of their clout through the years is another matter of debate.

Reeves says injunctions are constantly evolving to accommodate changes in gangs and changes in the law, and that he has no intention of letting up on the pressures that injunctions place on gang members, as long as his budget allows.

While today's gang injunctions are more tightly written, heavily documented and resistant to constitutional challenge than in previous years, some, including Chief Batts, say they may have worked better in the early years, when they caught gangsters off guard. Now, the gang members know what the injunctions do, how they work and how to undermine them.

"What we do today will be antiquated tomorrow," Batts says. "Guys working on the street are extremely creative. You find a mousetrap, and they find a loophole in that mousetrap."

He says he wouldn't be surprised if injunctions become obsolete someday.

"It will only be good for a finite amount of time," he says. "Someday, we will have to change our tactics."

Periodical Bibliography

The following articles have been selected to supplement the diverse views presented in this chapter.

Gregory J. Boyle
"Gang Bill Panders to Irrational Fear; the Problem Is Social, Not a Matter for Law Enforcement," *Los Angeles Times*, December 18, 2003.

Congressional Digest
"Loitering and Individual Rights," *Supreme Court Debates*, February 1999.

Terry Costlow
"A Town Fights Gangs by Obtaining Right to Sue Them," *Christian Science Monitor*, May 20, 2002.

Susan Estrich
"Defining Criminal Behavior," *Liberal Opinion Week*, July 5, 1999.

Heike P. Gramckow and Elena Tompkins
"Enabling Prosecutors to Address Drug, Gang, and Youth Violence," *JAIBG Bulletin*, December 1999.

Tom Hayden
"Gato and Alex—No Safe Place—Gangs and State Violence: The Human Story of the Los Angeles Police Scandal," *Nation*, July 10, 2000.

Lonnie Jackson
"Understanding and Responding to Youth Gangs: A Juvenile Corrections Approach," *Corrections Today*, August 1999.

Ember Reichgott Junge
"Assistant U.S. Attorney Works to Prosecute Gangs, Leaders," *Minnesota Lawyer*, January 27, 2003.

Thomas M. Keane
"Anti-Loitering Laws Aren't Gang-Busters," *Boston Herald*, March 26, 2003.

Bill Lockyer
"Blueprint to Reduce Youth Gang Violence," *Business Journal*, May 2, 2003.

Terry McCarthy
"The Gang Buster," *Time*, January 19, 2004.

O. Ricardo Pimentel
"Gang Injunctions Trample Some Basic Rights," *Arizona Republic*, June 13, 2000.

Lawrence Rosenthal
"Gang Loitering and Race," *Journal of Criminal Law & Criminology*, Fall 2000.

Frank Salvato
"Gang Violence: The Ultimate Denial of Free Speech," *Washington Dispatch*, October 28, 2003.

Nina Siegal
"Ganging Up on Civil Liberties," *Progressive*, October 1997.

Heather Slater	"Anti-Loitering Laws Asked to 'Move Along,'" *OpinionEditorials.com*, April 18, 2003.
Jacob Sullum	"Sweeping Powers," *Reason*, October 14, 1998.
Joseph Trevino	"Politics in the Street: The Debate That Matters on Gang Injunctions," *LAWeekly*, May 25–31, 2001.

CHAPTER 4

What Can Be Done to Address the Problem of Gangs?

Chapter Preface

Many communities in the United States have confronted the problems of gangs and gang violence. While some locations have focused on increased police actions and crackdowns on crime, other communities have utilized solutions outside of law enforcement. In the 1990s Boston, Massachusetts, began a multipronged approach to gangs; its story serves both as an inspiration and a cautionary tale for other cities seeking to solve the problem of gang violence.

In 1990 the problem of gang violence in Boston had reached a critical point. An estimated thirty-five to forty street gangs had more than four thousand members in the city of 550,000. Three-quarters of the city's 152 homicides that year were gang-related. Boston responded by developing a multifaceted program involving a coalition of law enforcement and social welfare personnel, university professors, and community and religious leaders. They developed several innovative programs that combined law enforcement with community welfare. In Operation Cease Fire, police met directly with identified gang leaders to tell them that violence and other crimes would be immediately met with swift sanctions and prosecutions. Operation Night Light had social workers, police, and probation officers working together to check up on at-risk youth at their homes. The Safe Neighborhoods Plan encouraged people to serve as role models in their neighborhoods. Religious leaders instituted programs in which counselors and ministers worked directly with at-risk youth. Boston police helped run day camps and worked with the Boys & Girls Clubs of Boston to provide children with alternative activities to gangs.

These and similar programs were, for a time, a stunning success. Both general and youth homicide rates greatly declined. By 1997 firearm homicides were down 90 percent compared to 1990 figures. In 1998 Boston had only twenty-three homicides. Other cities looked to Boston as an example of how to solve the problem of gang violence.

More recently, however, gang violence has been on the rise in Boston. Its homicide rate rose to sixty-six in 2001 and sixty the following year. Nine Bostonians were killed in the first six weeks of 2004—many of those homicides were apparently gang-related. Various theories have been offered to account for the resurgence of violence. Some observers argued that gang-affiliated criminals imprisoned in the 1980s and 1990s were coming back on the streets. Other commentators blamed the spread of gangs from other cities including Los Angeles. But many observers have argued that Boston's initial success laid the seeds for eventual failure—as the problem of gang violence decreased, the community efforts to combat gangs lost their intensity. "I'm not saying we got lazy, but we lost focus," concluded Philip J. Carver, president of a neighborhood association in Boston. "Once we took the higher echelon of gang leaders out, we became lax."

Boston's experience shows that the search for solutions to the problem of gangs is a lengthly and perhaps never-ending process. The viewpoints in this chapter provide various ideas on how communities can respond to gangs in their midst.

*"What if everyone worked for full
employment instead of full
incarceration?"'*

Communities Should Provide Economic and Social Support for Potential and Past Gang Members

Martin McHugh

Martin McHugh was a writer and editor of *Company*, a magazine produced by and for members of the Roman Catholic religious order the Society of Jesus (Jesuits). The following viewpoint describes the work of Greg Boyle, a Jesuit priest who for years has worked in gang-affected parts of Los Angeles, California. Boyle has founded various organizations that provide jobs and other forms of support to impoverished and high-risk youth, many of whom have gang affiliations or backgrounds. It is only by providing such support and hope for the future away from gangs that the problem of gangs will be solved, Boyle and McHugh believe.

As you read, consider the following questions:

1. How does McHugh describe the neighborhood in which Greg Boyle works?
2. What are some of the businesses in Los Angeles that have employed former gang members, according to the author?
3. What message does Boyle want to send to government officials, according to McHugh?

Martin McHugh, "Homeboy," *Company Magazine*, Fall 1998. Copyright © 1998 by *Company Magazine*. Reproduced by permission.

S tart-ups. Spin offs. Venture cap. Burn rate. R&D. Ramping up. You hear buzzwords such as these wherever people are engaged in business. There is one spot in East Los Angeles, however, where the word ministry also has a place in the commercial lexicon.

Dolores Mission, a Jesuit ministry in a predominately Latino neighborhood in East L.A., is the poorest parish in the archdiocese. Poverty there is as much a part of the economic landscape as housing projects are of the physical environment. Gang activity weaves its way through daily life there. You would be hard pressed to find anyone whose life has not been affected by turf wars, drive-by shootings, or drugs. Many youth in the area are considered "high risk," likely to suffer from or take part in gang violence and end up in the hospital, doing time, or worse.

But Fr. Greg Boyle, SJ, who has been at Dolores Mission and working in its community outreach program, Proyecto Pastoral, for ten years, knows of a lure for these youth stronger than that of the easy money the drug trade offers: that of honest work. Boyle has met so many for whom dollars earned from painting or cleaning or hauling are all the sweeter for being earned honestly, with dignity. He has dedicated a phenomenal amount of effort to capitalizing on this knowledge and pointing out to others in the neighborhood the possibility of having a future "out of the life," out of the world of gangs and violence.

Jobs for a Future

One of Proyecto Pastoral's programs is Jobs For A Future (JFAF), an employment referral center. "Finding people looking for work is never a problem. Jobs For A Future is pretty well known around here," says Boyle. "Those who come through the doors are young men and women between 13 and 25, many with a gang past, and most whom we consider to be high risk." Some who come have just been released from one of the fourteen detention centers where Boyle works as a chaplain; they know ahead of time where to go to get help turning their lives around.

JFAF gets jobs for them at a variety of places, including many factories, Macy's, United Parcel Service, and production companies in "the business," as the movie industry is referred to in L.A.

"It's the best," says Boyle, "when you get a call from a company who wants another employee 'just like Carlos, who you sent us last week.'" Call-backs like that are not the only source of placements. Two full-time staffers work the phones, making cold calls, explaining their service to prospective employers and asking them to keep JFAF in mind for their needs. As well, some personnel departments call to ask JFAF to fill a position; there are even some employment agencies who ask JFAF to find someone for a position they are unable to fill.

Developing this job referral network took time and effort, but it works. JFAF has been placing people in positions at a rate of 250 per year, and "We'll go over that number this year [1999]," says Norma Gillette, job development supervisor.

JFAF's work with clients starts with counseling, mentoring, and even free tattoo removal, but it does not stop once a client is hired. "We do a lot of follow-up, maintaining contact with both employer and employee," says Boyle. JFAF might call up a new hire who they learn has not shown up to work for a couple of days. "He might tell us, 'Yeah. I broke up with my lady,' Boyle says, "and then you help him deal with that. It's a matter of helping him keep the chaos in his life at bay."

Creating Jobs

A growing part of Proyecto Pastoral's activities has been in actually creating jobs as well as finding them. Homeboy Industries, founded in 1992, is an umbrella "corporation" for a growing number of affiliated works. One of them, Homeboy Bakery, started a few years ago to give work to former gang members, many from rival gangs. But the tortillas they were making and marketing ran into stiff competition, so much so that the business foundered and actually closed shop for a while.

A $160,000 grant from radio station KPWR's foundation, "Knowledge is Power," got the bakery back on its feet; a partnership agreement with Frisco Baking Co., which needed more production to fill its orders for French and

Italian bread from L.A. restaurants, gave Homeboy Bakery a fresh start.

Care Gould, who taught at the Dolores Mission Alternative School while a member of the Jesuit Volunteer Corps, now supervises Homeboy Bakery, one twenty-pound bag of flour and one block of yeast at a time. But those bags and blocks add up during daily production runs.

Invest in Childhood Education

A large number of little children in America lead miserable lives. Within less than two decades, many of these children become the core group of high-rate violent criminals. A crime control strategy that relies exclusively on punishing criminals and puts no effort into helping children is short-sighted both practically and morally. Empirical evidence strongly suggests that heavy spending on high-quality early childhood education is cost-effective and crime-reductive. . . .

There is much that remains uncertain about programs to help young children. However, investing social resources in a variety of experimental programs, no matter how expensive they are, is likely to bear better fruit than proven failures such as gun control and gang control. Incarcerating criminals is not a proven failure, since incarceration at least keeps the particular criminal from harming anyone except fellow prisoners. But does it not make more sense to help parents and children today, knowing that a child who can enjoy a better childhood is much less likely to need incarceration, at great taxpayer expense, when he becomes a teenager?

David B. Kopel, *Barry Law Review*, 2000.

"Not too long ago we were producing 600 loaves a day. That went up to 1,500 loaves a day," says Care. "Now we're at 3,000. And we're expecting to get new equipment that will allow us to double that production."

Doubling production will mean more employment for people who need it. "Right now we have eight full-time employees, most of them coming from gang backgrounds," says Care, "I'd characterize all of them as coming from high-risk backgrounds. We look for people willing to put aside former gang differences and concentrate on redirecting their lives, and we've gotten them from Jobs For A Future."

"Homeboy Silk-Screen did about $500,000 in business

last year (1997); right now we're $140,000 ahead of where we were last year at this time," says Ruben Rodriguez, a former Homeboy Bakery employee. He and his wife, Cristina, have been in partnership with Homeboy Industries and running the operation from its start. . . .

Homeboy Silk-Screen prints and ships T-shirts for radio stations, schools, and record labels, including Rhino, A&M, and Geffen. "Everyone from mom-and-pop stores to some of the major players in the entertainment world are our customers," says Ruben. He and Cristina oversee a staff of fourteen. "They've all come to us from Jobs For A Future."

It was a $50,000 grant from radio station KPWR that got Homeboy Silk-Screen going. Ruben and Cristina supplied the motivation: "Fr. Greg's message is simple: 'Jobs, not Jail.' We've seen it work," says Ruben. . . .

The Future

Boyle and his work on behalf of L.A.'s Latino youth have been the subject of a book and numerous newspaper and magazine articles as well as segments on *60 Minutes* and the *Today* show. That type of national publicity never hurts, but Boyle concentrates more on the local scene; that is where he finds jobs and clients.

"He's busy two or three times a week speaking at conferences, talking to groups of teachers and social workers, letting them know what Homeboy does," says Norma Gillette. Boyle does not ask for donations at these talks, but they come, along with names of further job contacts on both sides of the fence, those looking for work and those looking for employees.

"What if everyone worked for full employment instead of full incarceration?" asks Boyle. "Jobs For a Future and Homeboy Industries are intervention programs aimed at youth, and I want these programs to be as symbolic as they are actual; I want to send a message to legislators and government officials that we either have to deal with the problem of urban violence or we're going to end up warehousing the consequences."

"The whole point is to put a face, a human face, on gang members," concludes Boyle, for whom the word ministry carries a lot of meaning.

> "*Gang violence is a societal problem, and all parts of our society play a role in tolerating and enabling it.*"

Communities Must Stand Up to Gang Intimidation

Paul Douglas White

Paul Douglas White is a teacher at West Valley Leadership Academy, an alternative school in Los Angeles. In the following viewpoint he argues that gang violence is a societal problem that is caused in part by a failure of intimidated parents and community residents to press charges against gang members or otherwise assist law and school authorities in fighting gangs. The problem of gangs will worsen unless more people make a commitment to stand up to the threat of gang violence, he concludes.

As you read, consider the following questions:

1. What does White call the ultimate problem behind gang violence?
2. What sorts of actions against gang members are taken at the school in which the author teaches?
3. What things do parents do that contribute to gang violence, according to White?

Paul Douglas White, "Freedom Is Never Risk-Free," *Los Angeles Daily News*, September 14, 2003, p. V1. Copyright © 2004 by *Los Angeles Daily News*, Los Angeles Newspaper Group. Reproduced by permission of the author.

[T]he] apparent gang shooting near Taft High School in Woodland Hills [in September 2003], which left three wounded, wasn't a tragedy—it was a miracle. It's miraculous that such attacks haven't been happening on a weekly basis, at countless Los Angeles-area schools, and with much more deadly results.

The growing problem of gang violence in Los Angeles and most major cities is not going to just go away. It's not going to blow over, quiet down or burn itself out.

It's not just kids being kids, but an unprecedented, out-of-control blaze of murder and mayhem, fed by moral cowardice and a dereliction of duty on the part of parents, schools, residents and merchants of infected neighborhoods.

The ultimate problem is that gang members are willing to die for the evil values they believe in, and the good guys who oppose them are not.

At the same time parents, communities and merchants decry gang activity and demand police protection, they obstruct law enforcement through their unwillingness—for fear of reprisals—to identify perpetrators and to press charges.

Firsthand Experience

This isn't just theory; I speak from experience. As a teacher at the West Valley Leadership Academy in Canoga Park, an alternative school site run by Los Angeles County, I've seen firsthand what it will take to win the war on gangs.

The West Valley Leadership Academy caters almost exclusively to repeat juvenile offenders, gang members and abusers of drugs and alcohol. Over a period of six years and at three different school sites, our buildings have a reputation for being spotless and graffiti-free. Gang violence, racial disputes and other crimes are virtually nonexistent.

Our students' behavior is so polite and gentle that, on public outings, we are often mistaken for a pricey private school. Our probation students' reoffending rate is less than one-third the norm.

What did it take to achieve this?

A willingness to do daily battle with gang members and stand up to their threats, intimidation and physical assaults at personal risk. A willingness to stand up to every single hint of lawless behavior with whatever legally available force or action is necessary and required.

Gang members caught defacing property inside or outside of our school are not just suspended or expelled; their parents are forced to pay for the damages. When gangsters not enrolled in our school have tried to enter the campus, they have been arrested on the spot by school officials, the police or both.

On a number of occasions, gang members who have refused to leave our building after being suspended have assaulted school personnel. As the law allows and requires, these students were immediately restrained by school staff until the police came. Then they were arrested, charged and incarcerated.

DIVIDED WE FALL; UNITED WE STAND.

Anderson. © by Kirk Anderson. Reproduced by permission.

This kind of proactive behavior is not risk-free. It can result—and has resulted—in injuries and threats to school personnel. But history offers no examples of freedom from tyranny being purchased without a price, and anyone who doesn't believe that gangs are successfully and increasingly tyrannizing Los Angeles is badly mistaken.

After establishing our reputation for not backing down, we have become well known to the gang members in our neighborhoods, known for our commitment to keeping our areas crime-free, and we almost never see them, because they prefer to locate in a neighborhood—like yours, perhaps?—where they can intimidate the local community residents and conduct their criminal activities in peace.

Too Much Tolerance

Gang violence is a societal problem, and all parts of our society play a role in tolerating and enabling it.

The parents of gang members are all too often tolerant or intimidated by their children's criminal activity and drug involvement. They provide shelter and food to their young hoodlums and their children's crime partners. They allow their troubled kids to drop out of school, and they lie to the police about their children's gang involvement.

Then, when their little victimizers become victims, they cry to the media and blame it on poor law enforcement.

The voices of community residents and merchants, railing against gang violence at endless public meetings and candlelight vigils, also ring hollow, because they, too, are often afraid to stand up and identify perpetrators, to press charges, to make citizens' arrests. They refuse to stand outside their homes and businesses armed with the most potent weapons in the fight against crime: cell phones and video cameras.

Problems of Schools

Schools, too, play a significant role in perpetuating this problem.

The Los Angeles Unified School District, like most major school districts, doesn't utilize the strong provisions of the Education Code to arrest and incarcerate gang members. Instead, it prefers the less provocative—and fiscally more attractive—approach of relocating them to "gangster clubhouses" (also known as alternative education sites).

There, the criminal gang subculture grows and flourishes. Teachers and administrators, for fear of being assaulted, tend to cower in the corners, enforce no behavioral or dress standards, and let the students run the school.

Our wonderful City of Angels and countless communities just like it across America will never be free from the grip of gang violence until we stop passively waiting for some public official or agency to take a much-needed moral stand. Each one of us must become willing to put up our own spirited resistance against this evil, in whatever form the situation might call for.

"A man who won't die for something is not fit to live," Martin Luther King once said. If the community residents in Los Angeles will make a life-or-death commitment to defending their children and communities from the gang scourge then they will enjoy—because they will have earned—the same sort of peaceful haven that we have at our school and in our neighborhood.

A Winnable Battle

This battle against Los Angeles' gang violence is winnable, as we've proven at our school, but each individual campus and neighborhood has to take a stand. No one can do it for you.

Gang shootings like the one at Taft High School will continue—and worsen—until more of us are willing to make the required radical commitment to stop the violence. Refusal to take such action will guarantee Los Angeles County a future that none of us would want to contemplate.

> "The medical community would lead a huge
> public outcry if an infectious agent caused
> morbidity and mortality comparable to
> that of gang violence."

Communities Should Treat Gang Violence as a Public Health Problem

Allen L. Hixon

Allen L. Hixon is a professsor of clinical family practice in the Department of Family and Community Medicine at the University of California, Davis, School of Medicine. In the following viewpoint he notes that joining a gang increases one's risk of violent death by 60 percent, and calls for health care professionals to take greater steps to respond to the problem of gang violence. For example, he recommends that health care workers provide tattoo removal services for gang members who wish to change their lives.

As you read, consider the following questions:
1. What makes gangs a pressing adolescent health problem, according to Hixon?
2. What examples of successful antigang community organizations does the author describe?
3. What role do family physicians have in the fight against gangs, according to Hixon?

Allen L. Hixon, "Preventing Street Gang Violence," *American Family Physician*, vol. 59, April 15, 1999, p. 2,121. Copyright © 1999 by the American Academy of Family Physicians. All rights reserved. Reproduced by permission.

A two-year-old child riding a tricycle dies, the random victim of a drive-by shooting. A pregnant woman is hit by a stray bullet in East Los Angeles. Street gang members storm the emergency department of an urban hospital to "finish off" a rival gang member. Are these random acts confined to the inner city? Is this media sensationalization, racial stereotyping or a realistic depiction of a major adolescent health epidemic sweeping U.S. cities and towns?

Several recent publications examine this public health problem, debunk some of the myths and move beyond the now commonplace stereotype of a gang member—a tattooed teenager in baggy pants, high-top sneakers and an athletic jacket. Important questions are raised. What is the connection between street gangs and violence? Who is at greatest risk? What role might family physicians and parents play in preventing gang violence?

Epidemiology

Street gangs have a presence in 94 percent of all U.S. cities with populations greater than 100,000. Los Angeles has over 950 different gangs with more than 100,000 members. One study performed in Chicago showed that 5 percent of elementary school children were affiliated with street gangs, as were 35 percent of high school dropouts. Gangs have upset school systems nationwide, as demonstrated by the now common use of dress codes, metal detectors and security guards. Gangs are not limited to inner-city ghettos but are active in over 800 cities nationwide. Alarmingly, nearly 100 cities with populations less than 10,000 report active street gangs.

It is the relationship of gangs to homicide that make this concern a pressing adolescent health problem. Gunshot wounds are the eighth leading cause of death in the United States. It is estimated that firearms are used in 80 to 95 percent of gang-related homicides. Membership in a street gang increases one's risk of violent death by 60 percent. This increased risk of mortality, as well as the proliferation of street gangs, should be of grave concern to health care professionals.

Street gangs have been described as an aggregation of youths who perceive themselves as distinct, who are viewed as distinct by their community and who call forth a consistently negative image of themselves through their actions. American street gangs have historically been ethnically based. Early American street gangs were Irish, Polish or Italian. In the 1950s and 1960s, African-American, Mexican and Puerto Rican gangs became prominent. While gangs have traditionally been male dominated, female involvement in gangs and all-female gangs are not uncommon.

During the past decade, African-American, Mexican, Hmong, Vietnamese, Chinese, and white gangs have been common; in recent years, Russian and American Indian gangs have been reported. Ethnic gangs develop their own gang culture and identity, which includes specialized nicknames, nonverbal communication, tattoos, style of dress, mannerisms and vocabulary. Mass media images, specifically pop music culture and television, have propagated many of these outward trappings, which have been adopted to a large extent by mainstream adolescent culture. In many cases, media images have sensationalized gang life and furthered racial stereotypes, complicating society's understanding of the real nature of the problem.

Characteristics of Gangs

Gangs have traditionally been territorially organized around a specific neighborhood, school or housing project. This geographic orientation has been at the root of intergang violence, and the function of the gang as a mode of protection has evolved. Terms such as "turf," "hood" and "barrio" describe the territorial basis of gangs. In-fighting is frequent between competing gangs of the same ethnicity. In fact, the majority of gang-related homicides are intra-racial.

Negative gang activities vary widely, ranging from truancy, fighting and vandalism to burglary, assault, homicide and extortion. The drug-gang connection is often cited, but many researchers believe this activity is overstated. While gangs form a continuum from groups of disgruntled adolescents to organized crime syndicates, most street gangs are not efficient or sophisticated drug distributors.

Gang membership is driven in part by the function of street gangs. Gangs are perceived as a source of protection in a violent world. Two major predictors of gang membership include residence in a gang-infested neighborhood and the presence of an older sibling who is already in a gang. Individual risk factors include status and identity needs, poverty, unemployment, dysfunctional families, ethnic segregation and inadequate education opportunities. Gangs function to give adolescents a much-needed sense of belonging and self-esteem in the transition to adulthood. Gangs may be viewed as a failure of society to socialize a segment of its youth.

Prevention Strategies

Prevention strategies focus on these risk factors and begin with an understanding of root causes, specifically, the breakdown of traditional family and community structures, lack of economic opportunity, racism and limited role models. Citizens and physicians may intervene by promoting active parenting and community organization. Parents must be taught to recognize signs of gang involvement in children, as well as constructive ways to respond.

Table 1: Screening Questions for Gang Involvement

Do you feel safe in your neighborhood/school?

What would you do if you needed protection?

Do you have access to a handgun?

What is the significance of your tattoo/your style of clothing?

Do you have friends or siblings who are involved in a gang?

Examples of successful community programs include "Mothers Against Gangs," an organization that mobilizes parents in preventing school delinquency. In addition to providing training in parenting skills, initiatives include computer literacy, homework tutors, youth entrepreneurship initiatives and legislative advocacy. Another program called "Youth Struggling for Survival" recognizes that gang life is organized around destructive rituals. Founded by a former gang member, this program attempts to bring at-risk youth together and to substitute new rituals, such as African traditions and Native American sweat lodges.

Alternative activities such as supervised evening sports programs have been implemented in many communities. "Cops in the Classroom" programs have been used as a method of making the initial contact with law enforcement a positive one. All of these interventions have had some success but must be implemented in ways that will not inadvertently increase gang cohesiveness. Factors that make gangs appear more visible, organized and relevant may have the undesired effect of attracting new gang members.

Family physicians also have a key role in working with school officials, law enforcement, social services and the local health department in efforts of community organization. In addition, physicians are in the unique position of treating individual adolescents in the context of the family, which in some cases has been functionally replaced by the gang.

Like domestic violence, gang involvement often will not be revealed unless it is actively sought. Adolescent screening should take place in the context of understanding local gang patterns. Screening should focus on high-risk behaviors such as drug and alcohol use, access to handguns, self-esteem issues, school delinquency and having a sibling involved in a gang [see Table 1]. Initiating counseling and support services for at-risk children is important, although counseling alone is unlikely to be beneficial without concurrent changes in the home and socioeconomic environments. . . .

Other useful interventions include referral to parenting skills classes, providing gun safety information, tattoo removal programs and emergency department crisis response teams. Understanding the significance of tattoos and providing laser tattoo removal when appropriate may change lives. A hospital-community response team with trained crisis counselors who are available for immediate intervention with gang members and their families may be developed and may help prevent retaliation crimes.

The Role of Doctors

The proliferation of street gangs in America, as well as the violence associated with gang activity, is alarming. Family physicians are in a unique position to focus community awareness on this major health problem of adolescence. The medical community would lead a huge public outcry if an infectious agent caused morbidity and mortality comparable to that of gang violence. We should demand nothing short of a national policy on violent street gangs with an appropriate commitment of public health resources. Our children deserve no less.

"Parents are not powerless, particularly when it comes to saving their kids from street gangs."

Parents Can Discourage Gang Involvement

Kendra Hamilton

Kendra Hamilton is assistant editor of the academic journal *Black Issues in Higher Education*. In the following viewpoint she focuses on the impact parents have in affecting their children's decision to join gangs. Hamilton examines the work of Chanequa Walker-Barnes, a psychology professor at the University of North Carolina at Chapel Hill. Walker-Barnes concluded from her research that parents—especially those in African American families—have much influence over their children and can help them avoid gangs.

As you read, consider the following questions:

1. What conclusion did the National Research Council reach in 1993 regarding parental influence over youth, according to Hamilton?
2. What sorts of questions were students asked by Walker-Barnes?
3. What differences did Walker-Barnes find between families of differing ethnic and racial groups, according to Hamilton?

Kendra Hamilton, "Gangbusters: Parents Still Play Key Role in Saving Kids from the Streets," *Black Issues in Higher Education*, July 4, 2002. Copyright © 2002 by CMA Publishing, Inc. Reproduced by permission.

There's a strong message to be taken from Dr. Chanequa Walker-Barnes' research, and it's simply this: Parents are not powerless, particularly when it comes to saving their kids from street gangs.

Indeed, the conclusions Walker-Barnes draws in her recent research project—examining ethnic differences in the effect of parenting on gang involvement and delinquency—fly in the face of long-accepted standards in her field. In 1993, for example, the National Research Council (NRC) stated that the impact of deviant peers is overwhelming during adolescence for African American youth—so much so that there may be nothing parents can do to offset it.

That just didn't sit well with Walker-Barnes, who is an assistant professor of psychology at the University of North Carolina-Chapel Hill. That was part of what got her into this area, she explains, while working on her dissertation at the University of Miami.

A sudden explosion of gang membership at her high school in Decatur, Ga.—a place that formerly had only seen "two fights a year," as Walker-Barnes describes it—piqued her curiosity about adolescent gang involvement. But it was the NRC's dismal pronouncement—combined with the urgings of her adviser, the University of Miami's Dr. Craig Mason—that sparked her interest in the interaction between parenting and peer relationships. "I began to ask myself what parents could do to offset the influence of negative peers," Walker-Barnes says.

The Study

Participants in Walker-Barnes' study were recruited from 13 ninth-grade English classes at a Miami high school. The initial sample included 300 students ranging in age from 13 to 18. Fifty-four percent of the students were Latino, mostly Cuban, but the sample also included kids from Central and South America. Another 25 percent were Black—African American, Jamaican and Haitian. And the rest of the students were White or "other."

The majority of the students—almost 60 percent—lived in intact families, while nearly 32 percent lived with their mothers. In a small number of cases, the students lived with their fathers (3.7 percent)—or with a grandparent or aunt (2.7 percent).

With stringent anonymity protocols in place, the students completed a series of questionnaires—a long baseline questionnaire with follow-ups every three weeks for the remainder of the school year. Some of the questions measured gang involvement—defined as hanging out with gang members, wearing gang colors on purpose, and flashing gang signs—as well as gang delinquency—spray painting gang symbols, taking part in a gang fight, and selling drugs for a gang. Still others measured the levels of parental involvement—or "behavioral control."

Parents Can End the Cycle of Violence

Gangs are violent. They intimidate and create fear. Gangs threaten the safety and integrity of our communities by harassing or hurting innocent residents, displaying graffiti, decreasing property values and driving out local business. Youth gangs take on various forms in different communities so there is no single solution. Gangs operate by tempting and seducing children into self-destructive behavior. However, if parents and other responsible adults work together to effectively meet our children's needs, we can end the cycle of violence.

Ultimately, parents can be the most active players in preventing and reducing gang problems. Learning everything about gangs and why youth join gangs can help you keep your children and neighborhoods safe.

Second Chance Youth Program, "Parent's Guide to Preventing Gang Involvement," www.scyp.org/parents.htm.

"Behavioral control, as I defined it, consisted in measuring the parent's involvement in decision making," says Walker-Barnes. "I asked a series of questions and the answers were based on a five-point scale, where the low end was 'I decide on my own,' the middle was 'my parents and I discuss it and we make the decision together,' and high end was 'my parents tell me what to do and don't discuss it with me.'"

Generally, Walker-Barnes says, "high" behavioral control has been associated with what's known in the psychological literature as "authoritarian parenting"—high strictness combined with a lack of warmth, which is generally considered highly undesirable parenting behavior.

"What I found was that higher levels of that kind of parenting in African American kids resulted in better behavior over time," Walker-Barnes says.

Ethnic Differences

Walker-Barnes says the finding was gratifying. "In doing the initial analyses, looking at parenting for the group overall, parenting seemed to have no effect. And that was really disappointing to me because I had hoped to be able to show that it had a positive effect even in the context of having negative peers," Walker-Barnes says.

"Basically what was happening was that the differences between the ethnic groups were 'washing each other out' in the overall analysis, making it look as if peers" had the overwhelming impact cited in the NRC's and other previous studies.

"It was breaking the data up by ethnic group that gave me the really strong, clear results," Walker-Barnes adds.

In general, Walker-Barnes says, her study showed the level of gang involvement decreasing over the course of the first year of high school, perhaps indicating that participation in gang activities is a temporary phenomenon for many students, providing a sense of security during the difficult transition from middle to high school.

It was among Black youth, however, that parenting behavior showed the strongest, most clearly measurable impact. Higher levels of "behavioral control" resulted in lower levels of gang involvement and delinquency in that population. Meanwhile, "lax" parenting and the use of "psychological control"—in laymen's terms, "guilt-tripping"—resulted in higher levels of gang involvement.

By contrast, higher levels of behavioral control were related to increases in delinquency and gang involvement among White/other youth, while lax parenting and psychological control appeared to have no impact on this population.

Among the largest population, Latino youth, the most effective parental strategy appeared to be the psychological control strategy. Higher levels of psychological control were associated with lower levels of gang involvement. Again, as with White/other youth, lax parenting failed to have the negative impact that it had on Black youth.

Interestingly, the level of gang delinquency remained relatively constant for the overall population, indicating that youth involved in more serious forms of gang behavior may require more serious forms of intervention in order to be saved.

Walker-Barnes' research was published, along with Mason as her coauthor, in a recent issue of the prestigious psychology journal *Child Development*. Her research proves "that parenting is not one size fits all."

"The important variable could be ethnicity or cultural background, it could be neighborhood or environment. But, depending on the context the family is in, what parents need to do in order to raise healthy children could be quite different," she says.

"Being in a gang can put you in jail and keep you from reaching your dreams."

Youths Must Take Individual Responsibility to Steer Clear of Gangs

Melissa Ezarik

Writer Melissa Ezarik argues in the following viewpoint that many teens join gangs for the sense of support and security they provide, only to find that the path they have chosen is a dangerous one that hurts their future. She includes advice on how teens can avoid gangs and provides examples of teens who have stayed away from gangs or have left them. Ezarik is features editor of *District Administration*, a magazine for school administrators. She has written numerous articles for *Career World* and other publications for young people.

As you read, consider the following questions:
1. What reasons did Ryan give for never considering joining a gang, according to Ezarik?
2. According to the National Youth Gang Center, how many gangs operate in the United States?
3. What advice does Ezarik give about how teens should respond when they are being recruited to join a gang?

Melissa Ezarik, "How to Avoid Gangs: Money, Power . . . Gang Life May Seem to Have Its Perks, but Its Price Tag Is High. Here's What You Can Do to Keep Your Life on Track," *Current Health 2*, vol. 28, March 2002, pp. 20–24. Copyright © 2002 by Weekly Reader Corp. Reproduced by permission.

Growing up in a gang-infested San Francisco neighborhood, Ryan Calle, now 20, might have chosen the gang life. It's a path that some of his friends took. After all, gang members feel a sense of power and belonging.

But Ryan says, "I was never in danger of joining a gang. The thought never crossed my mind." While it was just he and his mom, who struggled to make ends meet, his circle of support got wider after a newspaper reporter shared their story with the community. One family even invited them to spend the holidays in their home each year.

"Love (and lots of it), encouragement, and being poor" were what Ryan thought each day. To impress his mom and the generous people who helped his family, his goal was to earn good grades. Ryan became even more determined after his mom died when he was 12. "Gangs could never mess with that," he says.

But many teens do join gangs. According to the National Youth Gang Center, there are 28,700 gangs with 780,200 active members in the United States. The U.S. Justice Department defines a gang as a group with a leader who issues orders and benefits from the gang's criminal activities. Most of these members begin hanging out with gangs at age 12 or 13, and within a year most have been arrested. So why do people join? The sense of family and acceptance they don't get elsewhere is one common reason. Gang life seems to provide support, security, and shared experiences. Boredom in school or after school is another reason. Kimo Souza, case management coordinator for the Mesa (Arizona) Gang Intervention Project, says that young people who join gangs are impressed by "all the things they lack and are looking for."

It's a myth that those who join gangs are always male and from low-income families in inner cities. The National Center for Education Statistics reports that in 1999, 25 percent of urban students, 16 percent of suburban students, and 11 percent of rural students reported a gang presence in their schools. Many gang members are from middle class families and are considered "good kids." In addition, one in 20 gang members is a female, and one-third of all gangs have a mixture of racial and ethnic groups. While some gang members wear certain colors, types of clothing, or tattoos, these signs of gang life are becoming less common.

Gang Life Is No Life

Gangs have a bad reputation—for good reasons. A National Youth Gang Center 11-city survey of eighth grade gang members found that more than 90 percent had engaged in violent behavior. To gain status and respect in a gang, you must be ready to defend fellow members. Going along with the group's decisions is another reason gang life is dangerous. Theft, burglary, assault, and robbery are common activities—and one-third of all gangs are organized for the purpose of drug trafficking. So being in a gang can put you in jail and keep you from reaching your dreams.

Getting in and out of a gang also tends to mean violence. The gang may require that new members be "jumped." To leave, you may have to get beaten up again, only often these beatings are much worse. Parents who urge their teens to get out of the gang life may also be targeted. Ryan adds, "Those who make it out might have to . . . live with the fact that they've stabbed or killed someone."

Standing Tough

To stay away from gangs, you may have to make tough choices. Here's a crash course in what to know and do:

• Understand how recruitment works. Intimidation is a traditional way of recruiting new gang members, but more subtle methods are becoming popular, says Steven J. Sachs in his book *Street Gang Awareness*. For example, gang members may tell you about the good things that gang life can offer. Then they befriend you—and before you realize it, you are one of them.

• Know how to respond to a gang member suggesting you join. Experts say that it's rare for gangs to hurt those who say no politely. You want to refuse to go along without making the person feel disrespected. For instance, you might say that your parents would ground you for life if they ever found out.

• Take your fears seriously. If a situation has made you uncomfortable, talk to a trusted adult, says Souza, whose gang intervention project helps prevent and reduce gang activity. Your parents, your friends' parents, teachers, principal, guidance counselor, religious leaders, and local police are there to help. Be honest and share your fears. Adults may know of solutions that you don't.

One Gang Member's Turnaround

On a steamy July night in 1996, Jeremy Greenwood stabbed a young man in a drunken rage and then ran away. At 16, the high school dropout was a fugitive, wanted on an attempted murder charge.

Today, the 18-year-old Greenwood has traded gangs, drugs and violence for a full college scholarship and plans to become a physician's assistant.

There are no miracles in Greenwood's turnaround, he says, just the faith of others and his own hard work. . . .

"The first step is wanting to change," he said. "Until you realize how bad off you are, until you make the conscious decision to change, you're not going to do anything. You're going to get sucked right back into the same stuff."

Michael G. Walsh, *Muskegon Chronicle*, November 19, 1998.

• Know your goals and values—and let them guide you in making decisions. What's important to you? Think about where you want to be in 10 years, five years, or even next month. Maybe you want to learn a new sport or make the honor roll. What do you believe in? Honesty, trust, and dependability are values you may hold dear. Say your friends want you to hurt someone or steal. How might going along affect your life? Souza suggests you trust your personal feelings and ask yourself, "Are these your friends? Is it really worth being with them?" Protect yourself.

• Surround yourself with positive peer pressure. Spend your time on activities that make you feel good—from sports or school clubs to community service or working. Souza says these activities offer a chance to create a new definition of the word "gang."

• Use common sense. The National Crime Prevention Council suggests avoiding dangerous shortcuts, staying in well-lit places at night, and walking with friends. Carry only the money you need; and if someone starts to follow you, find an area with a lot of people. Also seek places where you feel safe hanging out, whether it's your bedroom or the basketball court.

• Realize that it is possible—but difficult—to get out of a gang. If your group makes you uncomfortable, don't be available for group activities. Souza says that gang members whose roles aren't prominent may be able to move away from the group slowly. The more you stand out, however, the more you'll be missed.

Christine's Story

Christine is one teen that Souza has seen leave the gang life. She got to know the Mesa project leaders, and soon they helped her realize that the leadership skills she had learned in the gang could be used for better pursuits. When her former friends threatened her, she went straight to the program's detectives who helped calm the situation. Now 17, Christine has spoken at national conferences and been interviewed by CNN and other television stations. Souza says that Christine's positive experiences have been enjoyable. The more she does, the more she wants to do.

When Ryan's friends eventually tired of the gang life thrills, he says they found they had "lost a lot of time in becoming who they want to be." While they were determined to have a successful future, getting into and doing well in college were far from easy. Some of his friends now work with inner-city teens, showing them why gang life doesn't pay.

"I just wish that more kids out there were stronger about their own [lives]," Ryan says. As a student at California State University in Sacramento, he has discovered the secret to success—"kindness and hard work toward the unity of all people." He hopes teens will "join a bigger gang, one called a nation."

Periodical Bibliography

The following articles have been selected to supplement the diverse views presented in this chapter.

Jonathan Bailey Jr.	"Leaders Must Stand Firm Against Gangs," *Syracuse Post-Standard*, June 1, 2003.
Anita Bartholomew	"The Gangbuster," *Reader's Digest*, November 2002.
Kathy Boccella	"Faith-Based Coalition Out to Save Youths and Fight Crime," *Philadelphia Inquirer*, July 9, 2001.
Gregory Boyle	"Gang Bill Panders to Irrational Fear," *Los Angeles Times*, December 18, 2003.
Doug Brunk	"FPs Help Gang Members Start Over," *Family Practice News*, July 1, 2003.
Gary Delgado	"Warriors for Peace," *ColorLines*, Winter 1999.
Economist	"God Meets Mammon; Employing Gangsters," October 20, 2001.
Lonnie Jackson	"Understanding and Responding to Youth Gangs: A Juvenile Corrections Approach," *Education Digest*, November 2000.
David Kennedy	"We Can Make Boston Safe Again," *Boston Globe*, July 15, 2002.
Paul Palango	"Danger Signs: How One Teen Salvaged Her Life," *Maclean's*, December 8, 1997.
Julia Randle	"From Menace to Mentor," *Chicago Reporter*, June 2003.
Luis J. Rodriguez	"Could Today's Gangbangers Be Tomorrow's Heroes?" *Los Angeles Times*, December 19, 2002.
Andrew P. Thomas	"From Gangs to God," *Wall Street Journal*, October 23, 1998.
Donna Ojanen Thomas and Valerie G.A. Grossman	"Prevent Gang Violence by Understanding the Culture," *RN*, December 2003.
James Diego Vigil	"Streets and Schools: How Educators Can Help Chicano Marginalized Gang Youth," *Harvard Educational Review*, Fall 1999.
Gary Yates	"New Thinking Can Help Defeat Gang Violence," *Los Angeles Times*, November 29, 2003.

For Further Discussion

Chapter 1

1. Mike Carlie asserts that people are shaped by their "individual knowledge and from knowledge gained from social interactions with other people." How do you think the individual knowledge of and social interactions with gangs experienced by Wesley McBride and Mike Carlie shape their views about gangs? Explain, citing from the texts.

2. Diane Schaefer argues that anecdotal evidence is insufficient to establish that gangs from large cities have invaded smaller communities. David M. Allender cites evidence of gangs in Indianapolis, Indiana. Do you think Schaefer would characterize Allender's evidence as anecdotal? Explain, citing from the viewpoint.

3. Many of the authors in this chapter express concern about the way the media portray gangs and gang life. While some are concerned that the media exaggerate gang violence, others claim that media portrayals romanticize gang life, motivating disenfranchised youth to join gangs. How do you think media portrayals of gangs could be improved? Explain.

Chapter 2

1. Many of the viewpoints in this chapter focus on gangs in California. The California Attorney General's Office, Crime and Violence Prevention Center argues that California's gangs have become models for gangs in the rest of the nation. Do you agree or disagree with that assessment? Defend your answer, citing from the texts.

2. Some gang experts have classified risk factors for gang activity as being either "push" or "pull." Young people can be "pushed" into gangs through outside forces, or can be "pulled" into the gang by what they see as attractive features of the gang lifestyle. Which of the causes discussed in this chapter would you categorize as "push" factors? "pull" factors? Which category do you think is most influential? Explain.

3. Mark D. Freado uses the story of just one person to make his arguments about what causes gang behavior. What are the strengths and limitations of this approach in presenting arguments, in your view? Explain your answer.

4. After reading Mike Carlie's argument, do you believe that government should take steps to prevent young people from seeing

media portrayals of gangs on television and in the movies? Why or why not?

Chapter 3

1. Dianne Feinstein argues that the national problem of gangs has gotten worse in recent years. Mariel Garza expresses agreement, but goes on to argue that this calls into question the law enforcement strategies espoused by Feinstein. Do you believe that Garza is correct, and that an acknowledgment of the worsening problems of gangs actually weakens Feinstein's position? Explain your answer.

2. Mariel Garza begins and ends her article with quotations from rapper and movie actor Ice-T. What are the main points she is attempting to make with these citations? Do you believe they add a sense of authenticity or validity to her arguments? Why or why not?

3. John Gibeaut sees the use of state and federal laws to prosecute gang members as a useful strategy to reduce gang violence. Ryan Pintado-Vertner and Jeff Chang claim that the laws used to target gangs criminalize minority youth. These authors have very different conceptions of what defines a gang member. How does this influence their viewpoints? Explain your answer, citing from the text.

4. Gang-ridden communities have a strong interest in eliminating gangs and restoring order to their neighborhoods. On the other hand, minority community members who are doing nothing illegal have an interest in dressing as they wish and assembling in the streets of their neighborhoods without fear of being detained or arrested by the police. What legal strategy discussed in this chapter do you think strikes the best balance between these competing interests? Explain.

Chapter 4

1. Both Martin McHugh and Paul Douglas White back up their arguments with examples of how community institutions have dealt with gangs. Which examples do you find most compelling? Explain, citing from the viewpoints.

2. Do you believe the methodology of Dr. Chanequa Walker-Barnes as described by Kendra Hamilton provides an accurate picture of youths and gangs? What other methods or sources of information do you believe might be equally or more useful for social scientists researching the question of why youth join gangs? Defend your suggestions.

3. The authors of this chapter point to different community actors as having responsibility for preventing young people from joining gangs. Melissa Ezarik points to youth themselves, Kendra Hamilton points to parents, and Allen L. Hixon points to doctors, while other authors point to law enforcement, schools, and community leaders. Discuss and rank according to responsibility who you believe to be most important in discouraging gangs: individual youth, families, schools, police, doctors, and society at large. Defend your rankings, citing arguments from the texts.

Organizations to Contact

The editors have compiled the following list of organizations concerned with the issues debated in this book. The descriptions are derived from materials provided by the organizations. All have publications or information available for interested readers. The list was compiled on the date of publication of the present volume; the information provided here may change. Be aware that many organizations take several weeks or longer to respond to inquiries, so allow as much time as possible.

American Civil Liberties Union (ACLU)
125 Broad St., 18th Fl., New York, NY 10004
(212) 549-2500 • fax: (212) 549-2646
e-mail: aclu@aclu.org • Web site: www.aclu.org
The ACLU is a national organization that works to defend Americans' civil rights as guaranteed by the U.S. Constitution. It opposes curfew laws for juveniles and others and seeks to protect the public-assembly rights of gang members or people associated with gangs. The ACLU publishes the biannual newsletter *Civil Liberties*.

Boys and Girls Clubs of America
1230 W. Peachtree St. NW, Atlanta, GA 30309
(404) 487-5700
e-mail: info@bgca.org • Web site: www.bgca.org
Boys and Girls Clubs of America supports juvenile gang prevention programs in its individual clubs throughout the United States. The organization's Targeted Outreach Delinquency Prevention program relies on referrals from schools, courts, law enforcement, and youth service agencies to recruit at-risk youths into ongoing club programs and activities. The clubs publish *Gang Prevention Through Targeted Outreach*, a manual designed to assist local clubs in reaching youngsters before they become involved in gang activity.

Center for the Study and Prevention of Violence (CSPV)
Institute of Behavorial Science
University of Colorado at Boulder
Campus Box 439, Boulder, CO 80309-0439
(303) 492-8465 • fax: (303) 443-3297
e-mail: cspv@colorado.edu • Web site: www.colorado.edu/cspv
The CSPV was founded in 1992 to provide information and assistance to organizations that are dedicated to preventing violence, particularly youth violence. Its publications include the paper "Gangs

and Adolescent Violence," and the fact sheets "Gangs and Youth Violence" and "Female Juvenile Violence."

Child Welfare League of America (CWLA)
440 First St. NW, Third Floor, Washington, DC 20001-2085
(202) 638-2952 • fax: (202) 638-4004
Web site: www.cwla.org

The Child Welfare League of America, a social welfare organization concerned with setting standards for welfare and human services agencies, works to improve care and services for abused, dependent, or neglected children, youth, and their families. It publishes information on gangs and youth crime in the bimonthly journal *Child Welfare* as well as in several books, including *Beating the Odds: Crime, Poverty, and Life in the Inner City* and *Girls in the Juvenile Justice System.*

John Howard Society of Alberta
2nd Floor, 10523-100 Ave., Edmonton, AB T5J 0A8 Canada
(780) 423-4878 • fax: (780) 425-0008
e-mail: info@johnhoward.ab.ca
Web site: www.johnhoward.ab.ca

The John Howard Society of Alberta is a nonprofit agency concerned with the problem of crime and its prevention, and works to encourage people in the community to play an active role in the criminal justice process. Its publications include the newsletter *The Reporter* and various reports and papers including *Gangs* and *Youth Crime in Canada: Public Perception vs. Statistical Information.*

National Gang Crime Research Center (NGCRC)
PO Box 990, Peotone, IL 60468-0990
(708) 258-9111 • fax: (708) 258-9546
e-mail: gangcrime@aol.com • Web site: www.ngcrc.com

The NGCRC is a nonprofit independent agency that conducts research on gangs and gang members and disseminates information through publications and reports. It publishes the *Journal of Gang Research.*

National Major Gang Task Force (NMGTF)
338 S. Arlington Ave., Suite 112, Indianapolis, IN 46219
(317) 322-0537 • fax: (317) 322-0549
e-mail: nmgtf@earthlink.net • Web site: www.nmgtf.org

The NMGTF's goal is to provide a centralized link for all fifty state correctional systems, the Federal Bureau of Prisons, major jails, law enforcement, and probation and parole officers throughout the nation. The task force accomplishes this mission by generating and maintaining the National Correction Informational Sharing System, which is available to gang prevention groups across the country. It publishes the monograph "From the Street to the Prison: Understanding and Responding to Gangs."

National School Safety Center (NSSC)

141 Duesenberg Dr., Suite 11, Westlake Village, CA 91362
(805) 373-9977 • fax: (805) 373-9277
e-mail: info@nssc1.org • Web site: www.nssc1.org

Part of Pepperdine University, the center is a research organization that studies school crime and violence, including gang and hate crimes, and that provides technical assistance to local school systems. NSSC believes that teacher training is an effective means of reducing these problems. Its publications include the book *Gangs in Schools: Breaking Up Is Hard to Do* and the *School Safety Update* newsletter.

National Youth Gang Center (NYGC)

Institute for Intergovernmental Research
PO Box 12729, Tallahassee, FL 32317
(850) 385-0600 • fax: (850) 386-5356
e-mail: nygc@iiir.com • Web site: www.iir.com/nygc

The National Youth Gang Center was developed by the Office of Juvenile Justice and Delinquency Prevention (OJJDP) to collect, analyze, and distribute information on gangs and gang-related legislation, research, and programs. Its publications include *The NYGC Bibliography of Gang Literature*. It also makes numerous gang-related articles accessible on its Web site and on *OJJDP's Gang Publication*, a CD-ROM that it distributes on request.

Office of Juvenile Justice and Delinquency Prevention (OJJDP)

810 Seventh Street NW, Washington, DC 20531
(202) 307-5911 • fax: (202) 307-2093
Web site: http://ojjdp.ncjrs.org

As the primary federal agency charged with monitoring and improving the juvenile justice system, the OJJDP develops and funds programs on juvenile justice. Through its Juvenile Justice Clearinghouse, the OJJDP distributes fact sheets, the annual *National Youth Gang Survey* and reports such as "Youth Gangs: An Overview" and "Gang Suppression and Intervention: Community Models."

Teens Against Gang Violence (TAGV)
1486 Dorchester Ave., Dorchester, MA 02124
(617) 825-8248
e-mail: teensagv@aol.com • Web site: www.tagv.org
Teens Against Gang Violence is a volunteer, community-based, teen peer leadership program. TAGV distinguishes between gangs that are nonviolent and those that participate in violence. Through presentations and workshops, the organization educates teens, parents, schools, and community groups on violence, guns, and drug prevention. It provides information about its programs on its Web site.

Web Sites

Into the Abyss: A Personal Journey into the World of Street Gangs
http://courses.smsu.edu/mkc096f/gangbook
This Web site maintained by sociologist Mike Carlie features the entire contents of his book *Into the Abyss* as well as additional articles, updates, and Web site links about street gangs.

National Alliance of Gang Investigators Associations (NAGIA)
www.nagia.org
This Web site is a creation of NAGIA, an organization of criminal justice professionals and organizations that works to promote and coordinate national antigang strategies. It includes an online library of articles and links to regional gang investigation organizations.

Streetgangs.com
www.streetgangs.com
This Web site, created and maintained by gang researcher Alejandro A. Alonso, a graduate student of geography at the University of Southern California at Los Angeles, Department of Geography, presents a history of gangs in Los Angeles. It is not intended to glamorize the street gang culture but to help parents, educators, and youth understand how and why the gang phenomena has become so persuasive. It includes news articles about gangs and an extensive bibliography of gang research.

The Coroner's Report
www.gangwar.com
The project of Steve Nawojczyk, a former coroner and a nationally recognized gang researcher, the Web site includes an overview of American gangs, information on gang graffiti, as well as other articles and links on youth gangs.

Bibliography of Books

Curtis W. Branch — *Clinical Interventions with Gang Adolescents and Their Families.* Boulder, CO: Westview, 1997.

Curtis W. Branch, ed. — *Adolescent Gangs: Old Issues, New Approaches.* Philadelphia: Brunner/Mazel, 1999.

Douglas Century — *Street Kingdom: Five Years Inside the Franklin Avenue Posse.* New York: Warner Books, 1999.

Meda Chesney-Lind and John M. Hagedorn, eds. — *Female Gangs in America: Essays on Girls, Gangs, and Gender.* Chicago: Lake View, 1999.

Ko-lin Chin — *Chinatown Gangs: Extortion, Enterprise, and Ethnicity.* New York: Oxford University Press, 1996.

Herbert C. Covey — *Street Gangs Throughout the World.* Springfield, IL: Charles C. Thomas, 2003.

G. David Curry and Scott H. Decker — *Confronting Gangs: Crime and Community.* Los Angeles: Roxbury Park, 2002.

Scott H. Decker, ed. — *Policing Gangs and Youth Violence.* Belmont: CA: Wadsworth/Thomson Learning, 2003.

Scott H. Decker and Barrik Van Winkle — *Life in the Gang: Family, Friends, and Violence.* New York: Cambridge University Press, 1996.

Sean Donohue, ed. — *Gangs: Stories of Life and Death from the Streets.* New York: Thunder's Mouth, 2002.

Finn-Aage Esbensen, Stephen G. Tibbetts, and Larry Gaines — *American Youth Gangs' at the Millennium.* Long Grove, IL: Waveland, 2004.

Mark S. Fleisher — *Dead End Kids: Gang Girls and the Boys They Know.* Madison: University of Wisconsin Press, 1998.

Gus Gedatus — *Gangs and Violence.* Mankato, MN: LifeMatters, 2000.

Arnold P. Goldstein and Donald W. Kodluboy — *Gangs in Schools: Signs, Symbols, and Solutions.* Champaign, IL: Research Press, 1998.

John M. Hagedorn — *People and Folks: Gangs, Crime, and the Underclass in a Rustbelt City.* Chicago: Lake View, 1997.

Arturo Hernandez — *Peace in the Streets: Breaking the Cycle of Gang Violence.* Washington, DC: Child Welfare League of America, 1998.

James C. Howell — *Youth Gangs: An Overview.* Washington, DC: U.S. Department of Justice, 1998.

C. Ronald Huff	*Criminal Behavior of Gang Members and At-Risk Youths.* Washington, DC: U.S. Department of Justice, 1998.
C. Ronald Huff, ed.	*Gangs in America III.* Thousand Oaks, CA: Sage, 2002.
Lonnie Jackson	*Gangbusters: Strategies for Prevention and Intervention.* Lanham, MD: American Correctional Association, 1998.
Karen L. Kinnear	*Gangs: A Reference Handbook.* Santa Barbara, CA: ABC-CLIO, 1996.
Malcolm W. Klein	*Gang Cop: The Words and Ways of Officer Paco Domingo.* Walnut Creek, CA: Altamira, 2004.
George W. Knox	*An Introduction to Gangs.* Peotone, IL: New Chicago School Press, 2000.
Louis Kontos, David Brotherton, and Luis Barrios, eds.	*Gangs and Society: Alternative Perspectives.* New York: Columbia University Press, 2003.
G. Larry Mays, ed.	*Gangs and Gang Behavior.* Chicago: Nelson-Hall, 1997.
Joan McCord, ed.	*Violence and Childhood in the Inner City.* New York: Cambridge University Press, 1997.
Richard C. McCorkle and Terance D. Miethe	*Panic: The Social Construction of the Street Gang Problem.* Upper Saddle River, NJ: Prentice-Hall, 2002.
Jody Miller	*One of the Guys: Girls, Gangs, and Gender.* New York: Oxford University Press, 2001.
Jody Miller et al., eds.	*The Modern Gang Reader.* Los Angeles: Roxbury, 2001.
Daniel J. Monti	*Wannabe: Gangs in Suburbs and Schools.* Cambridge, MA: Blackwell, 1994.
Chester G. Oehme III	*Gangs, Groups, and Crime: Perceptions and Responses of Community Organizations.* Durham, NC: Carolina Academic Press, 1997.
Susan A. Phillips	*Wallbangin': Graffiti and Gangs in L.A.* Chicago: University of Chicago Press, 1999.
Fred Rosen	*Gang Mom.* New York: St. Martin's, 1998.
Steven L. Sachs	*Street Gang Awareness: A Resource Guide for Parents and Professionals.* Minneapolis: Fairview, 1997.
Randall G. Shelden, Sharon K. Tracy, and William B. Brown	*Youth Gangs in American Society.* Belmont, CA: Wadsworth/Thomson Learning, 2004.

James F. Short Jr.	*Gangs and Adolescent Violence.* Boulder, CO: Center for the Study and Prevention of Violence, 1996.
Gini Sikes	*Eight Ball Chicks: A Year in the Violent World of Girl Gangsters.* New York: Anchor Books, 1997.
Irving A. Spergel	*The Youth Gang Problem: A Community Approach.* New York: Oxford University Press, 1995.
Mark D. Totten	*Guys, Gangs, and Girlfriend Abuse.* Orchard Park, NY: Broadview, 2000.
Al Valdez	*Gangs: A Guide to Understanding Street Gangs.* San Clemente, CA: LawTech, 2000.
Valerie Wiener	*Winning the War Against Youth Gangs: A Guide for Teens, Families, and Communities.* Westport, CT: Greenwood, 1999.
Lewis Yablonsky	*Gangsters: Fifty Years of Madness, Drugs, and Death on the Streets of America.* New York: New York University Press, 1997.

Index

need for a new approach to, 113–15
need for increased national, 110
need for new techniques by, 144
problems with, 21–22
refinement of tools used by, 118
see also antiloitering ordinances; gang injunctions; police officers
Lawson, Scott, 63
legal issues/proceedings
attacking loyalty of gang members and, 117–18
defendant vs. witness rights and, 105
use of federal statutes for, 119–20
use of informants for, 120–22
witness testimony and, 105–106
legislation
addressing social problems vs., 114–15
advantages of using, 119–20
antidrug, 126–27
criminalizing gang acts, 129–30
need for federal, 110
con, 113, 114
tough stance on juvenile crime and, 128–29
unfairly targets youth of color, 131–32
see also antiloitering ordinances; gang injunctions
Lipuma, Frank, 121–22
Lizarraga, Ricardo, 108
Long, Patrick Du Phuoc, 82
Los Angeles area
gang homicide in, 80
gang migration from, 108–109
history of gangs in, 80–81, 100–101
injunctions in, 152
number of gang members in, 113, 144
number of gangs in, 20, 80, 108, 176
public nuisance laws in, 122–23
Los Angeles Police Department (LAPD), 16, 22
Los Angeles Sheriff's Department, 22
Los Angeles Unified School District, 173
Los Puenteros (gang), 73–74

Major, Aline K., 121
Marshall, Scott, 146
Maxson, Cheryl, 159
McBride, Wesley, 16, 18, 19, 113–14
McCaffrey, Barry, 126–27
McCollum, Bill, 127
McHugh, Martin, 165
media
contagion effect of crime/gang portrayals by, 30

define/create reality, 25
ignores link between gangs and social problems, 29
inaccurate portrayals of minority youth by, 28
increased coverage of gang-related subject matter by, 33
influences young people to join gangs, 96–98
misportrayal of gangs by, 33–34
obsession with violent crime by, 27–28
public attitudes on gangs influenced by, 26–27
social policy and, 30–31
Melbourne (Australia), 26
Mexican gangs, 101
migration. *See* gang migration
Moore, Demario, 108
Moore, Joan, 65, 77
Morales v. City of Chicago, 147–48
Mosk, Stanley, 147, 148
"Mothers Against Gangs" (community program), 178
MS (Mara Salvatrucha) (gang), 70

National Alliance of Gang Investigators Associations, 22, 49
National Center for Education Statistics, 187
National Research Council (NRC), 182
National Youth Gang Center, 22, 50, 51, 187
Native American communities
gang-related violence in, 58–59
ill-equipped police force for, 59–60
rise of gang culture in, 56–58
NDIC National Street Gang Survey Report, 53
New, Kenneth E., 118
New York City, 135
Nicaragua, 73–74

O'Connor, Sandra Day, 148
Office of Community-Oriented Policing Services (COPS), 33
Operation Cease Fire, 163
Operation Night Light, 163
Operation Weed and Seed, 33
O'Reilly, Bill, 97

parents
can help end cycle of violence, 183
study on ethnic differences among, 182–85
Peeler, Russell, 105
People ex rel. Gallo v. Acuna, 145

205

DATE DUE

MAR 17 2006			
MAY 18 2006			
NOV 8 2006			
DEC 17 2006			
MAR 29 2007			
APR 28 2007			
NOV 21 2007			
12-14-07			
JAN 14 2010			
			Printed in USA

HIGHSMITH #45230